THE FIRST AMENDMENT

THE
First Amendment

THE HISTORY OF
RELIGIOUS FREEDOM
IN AMERICA

William H. Marnell

DOUBLEDAY & COMPANY, INC.

GARDEN CITY, NEW YORK

LIBRARY OF CONGRESS CATALOG CARD NUMBER 64–16556
COPYRIGHT © 1964 BY WILLIAM H. MARNELL
ALL RIGHTS RESERVED
PRINTED IN THE UNITED STATES OF AMERICA

–

To Clare, Mother, and Mary

Contents

Introduction

This book arose from a conviction that the relationship of Church and State in the United States is not what current controversy sometimes makes it, that there is a deep and usually disregarded relationship between the Christian Church and the American State, that this relationship is one of the fundamental facts of American life, and that its changes are few and slow. Under the waves is the ocean, and under the final escarpment is the mountain; and both are deep, hidden, and fundamental.

There are two pronouncements about that relationship habitually recalled when the storm of passing controversy arises. One is contained in the First Amendment to the Constitution of the United States: "Congress shall make no law respecting an establishment of religion, or prohibiting the free exercise thereof." The other is Thomas Jefferson's comment on this amendment made in 1802 to a committee of the Danbury (Conn.) Baptist Association: "I contemplate with sovereign reverence that act of the whole American people which declared that their legislature should 'make no law respecting an establishment of religion, or prohibiting the free exercise thereof,' thus building a wall of separation between Church and State." Both the law and the commentary have that final importance which belongs to whatever molds the thought, confirms the will, and guides the action of a people. But the corollary to that importance is the necessity of understanding what the law and the commentary say and do not say.

This importance is all the greater at the present time because the passage of more than a century and a half has blurred the meaning of both. How many Americans today can define with reasonable accuracy the term *an establishment of religion*? There is a certain gaseous quality in words and phrases. They have an instinct for expansion, and the price they pay for expansion is dilution. Today the prohibition of an establishment of religion means the prohibition of the use of public funds and facilities for the furtherance of the work of a church. It takes its characteristic form in the prohibition of instruction in religious doctrine in the classrooms of public schools and, quite frequently, in the denial of rides in public school buses to children who attend church-supported schools. Now the clearest thinker of the eighteenth-century Enlightenment might have had the power of scientific prophecy to envisage a public school bus, but neither he nor the subtlest theologian of the eighteenth century could ever have envisaged the presence of a parochial school child on that bus as "an establishment of religion." They could fail to catch the last faint, evanescent whiff of the expanded gas, not because they did not know what an establishment of religion was but because they did.

An established church in the historic sense is a church supported by civil authority. In this definition *supported* is an undiluted term; it does not mean protected, encouraged, given moral or even financial support. It means that the church is an integral part of the state and receives from the state support appropriate to its nature as an integral part. An *establishment of religion* in the historic sense is the creation of an established church. The First Amendment, which ordains that "Congress shall make no law respecting an establishment of religion, or prohibiting the free exercise thereof," forbids Congress to bring into being an established church. Since the existence of an established church has tended throughout history to limit the free exercise of religion, the second phrase of the amendment reinforces the first. But the Bill of Rights was written to limit and define the powers of the federal government; only by extension and interpretation has it been applied to the states and to state government. When the First Amendment was adopted, three states—New Hampshire, Massachusetts, and Connecticut—did have an established church. In four others—Virginia, the Carolinas, and Georgia—the memory of a very different established church was extremely recent. Sometimes the reconciliation of opposites is best effected by a flat prohibition. Later, when the opposites have ceased to exist and the prohibition remains, time blurs its reason for existence and men change the foundation on which it rests. Such has been the fate of the First Amendment. It was passed, not because a majority of the delegates were necessarily opposed to an established church as a matter of principle, but because a ban on the principle of establishment was part of the price for a federal union.

It seems, then, that a review of the background and history of Church and State in America might have some value for the historical perspective it can provide. We are not primarily interested in the current skirmishes so hotly contested about the ideological outposts. Perhaps a legalistic subtlety prohibits religious instruction in a public school building but permits religious services at military and naval installations by chaplains of the several faiths who hold commissions in the armed services. But one suspects that the subtlety involved is not one of abstract philosophy but of concrete public policy. The great majority of Americans believe that the members of the armed services are entitled at public expense to the strengthening influence of religion and its consolations. Therefore we have co-operation by the State with the Church in this regard. Happily the affairs of the American people are not conducted in a spirit of bloodless logic, and public policy has a slow and certain way of modifying and formulating itself anew.

The American relationship of Church and State is the product of many forces, some of which operated in a very distant past. What the Middle Ages believed, what the Renaissance believed, what the dominant figures of the Reformation believed, what the thinkers of the Enlightenment believed, all have helped to determine what the American has believed. In our first two chapters we shall try to analyze these European patterns of belief. But most important has been what the American himself has believed. To analyze this is our real concern.

Public policy in America is seldom if ever the end product of belief alone. There is a strongly pragmatic bias to the American temperament, and Americans tend to react to facts more sensitively than to ideas. The factual relationship of Church and State in America has not been the result of the First Amendment to the Constitution; rather, the First Amendment to the Constitution was the result of a factual relationship rapidly solidifying when the Constitution was amended by the Bill of Rights. That factual relationship was part of the broader relationship brought into being by the newly formed union. Before the Revolution there were thirteen colonies united under the British Crown but not united with one another. In the New England colonies, except Rhode Island, the Puritan tradition was all-powerful and the establishment of the Congregational Church an almost unchallenged fact. In the southern colonies the Anglican

tradition existed and with it the establishment of the Anglican Church. In the middle colonies religious diversity was
the tradition. But by the latter half of the eighteenth century the Anglican superiority in the South was gravely
challenged by the dissenter churches, and in New England
the Congregational theocracy was rapidly passing into history. Not only was there a religious cleavage between New
England and the South, but religious cleavages were developing in the very regions where religious conformity had
been strongest. A common denominator of agreement on
the problem of religious establishments had to be discovered
as part of the price of union. That there be no national
establishment of religion was the only conceivable one.
That the state establishments should wither on the vine was
the inevitable corollary.

The First Amendment, then, was not the product of
indifference toward religion. It was not the product of the
deism which prevailed in the Enlightenment, however much
the spirit of deism may have been present in certain of the
Founding Fathers. Above all, it was not the product of
secularism, and to translate the spirit of twentieth-century
secularism back to eighteenth-century America is an out-
rage to history. The First Amendment was rather a logical
outcome of the Protestant Reformation and its ensuing
developments. It was so far removed from secularism as to
be the product of its exact opposite, the deep-seated concern of a people whose religious faith had taken many
forms, all of them active, all of them sincerely held. It was
so far removed from indifference toward religion as to be
the result of its antithesis, the American determination that
the diversity of churches might survive the fact of political
union.

The "wall of separation between Church and State" was
not and could not be a Chinese Wall to separate the eternal
and the temporal. The real relationship between Church and

State, in America and in every country where religion is strong, is a thing of the spirit, the infusion of the spirit of religion into the ordering of the affairs of society. A wall of separation which would bar that spirit from making itself felt in secular concerns can never be built, because it would have to bisect the human heart.

THE FIRST AMENDMENT

1

The Legacy of the Middle Ages

The Middle Ages, true to their principle of expressing things in final terms even at the expense of detailed accuracy, proclaimed that society was single and universal. On the spiritual side that single universality was achieved in a Catholic Church; on the material side in what was considered a perpetuation of the Roman Empire. The Church and State were one and inseparable in God's immutable order of things, but this does not mean that there was a State Church or a Church-State. Rather, in the ideal medieval concept the Church and the State were inseparable by the fact of parallelism, not the fact of identity.

The traditional statement of their relationship dates back to the fifth century and was the work of Pope Gelasius I (A.D. 494), as phrased in a letter to the Emperor Anastasius: "There are two principles whereby this world is chiefly ruled, the pontifical authority and the royal power. The authority of the priests is the more important in that at the Last Judgment they are to answer to the Lord for the kings themselves."[1]

To illustrate the concept Pope Gelasius offered an abundance of analogies and parables. The world is prefigured in Melchizedek, at once priest and king, and in David, who was prophet and king. It is allegorized in the greater and the lesser light, the sun and the moon. It is symbolized in the union of soul and body, a better analogy, since the soul is immortal, even as the Church, and the body is not, not even when the body is the Roman Empire. That the parallel extend but so far and then the Church continue alone through eternity is essential to the concept.

It is of the essence of parallels not to intersect. In the ideal medieval view of the matter, just as in the view of the current Supreme Court, Church and State do not intersect; each has its province and each should remain within it. But just as parallel lines extended far enough appear to converge, so such mighty parallels as the medieval Church and State first appeared to converge and then in large measure did converge. The empire, in actuality brought into being by Charlemagne in 800 but in theory a perpetuation of the Roman Empire, was destined to grow into the medieval Imperium, with its culture that was in part secular and in part religious. The Pope was its spiritual head, the Emperor its temporal head, but the power of coronation rested with the Pope. The distinction between *imperium Romanum* and *imperium Christianum* become increasingly theoretical, and the unity of Christendom carried increasingly as its corollary the unity of the Christian empire. There were one Church and one Empire, and in combination they were Christendom.

By the time of Pope Gregory VII (Hildebrand) the fusion was complete. The decree of 1075 forbidding lay investiture, the formal installation of prelates by secular princes, had implications far transcending the surface one. No right-minded person could object to the surface intention; it was to stop the sale of church positions. The effect beneath the surface assumes its magnitude from the magnitude of the landholdings of the bishops and abbots throughout Western Europe. As tenants these ecclesiastics were vassals of their princes, but with control of their appointment passing from prince to Pope by the ban on lay investiture the royal power over them was largely canceled. The surface problem of lay investiture was settled fairly soon and by a rational compromise; the problems beneath the surface, the problem of the boundary between Church and State, grew inveterate and great. That was the core problem of medieval political life.

THE RIGHTS OF THE POPE

The Catholic thesis is that the Pope is the vicar of Christ on earth and the visible head of the Church. Gregory added that the Pope had the right, which arose from his duty as the vicar of Christ, to judge and punish with ecclesiastical punishments even princes who transgressed the law of God. That Pope Gregory could do it was proved when a penitent Emperor stood barefoot for three days in the snow at Canossa, seeking an audience. But it was not part of the thesis that the Church subordinate the State nor in any degree hold it captive. The Church and State were one and universal, with two governments in their unity. Society itself remained unchanged, though the power of one government might grow and the power of the other dwindle. Society itself remained one and undivided, and its every member had to remain acceptable to both governments. The man excommunicated by the spiritual government lost his civil rights as a certain corollary. One either was inside, fully inside, or one was outside in exterior darkness.

By the time of the Fourth Lateran Council, which was convoked by Pope Innocent III in 1213 and opened on No-

vember 11, 1215, the two perfected societies were as completely synthesized as their natures would permit. The spiritual and the secular orders remained independent each in
its sphere, but the Pope as the head of Christendom possessed what a historian of the church councils terms "a
directive authority, peculiarly his own, over the emperor and
the other secular powers and thus over all Christians.
Christ's representative had become the crowning head of
the whole of Christendom, of an organism vitalized by
religious impulses, combining *imperium* and *sacerdotium* in
one universal community."[2] The High Middle Ages had
reached their zenith.

It is not for the twentieth century, leaning on the uncertain reed of mutual defense and striving with no deeper
unifying principle than the need of physical security to create
unity in the free world, to look with disdain at this concept
of a single universal society, perfected in its two parts
and motivated by a single set of principles expounded
ultimately by a single authority who speaks as vicar of God.
In the High Middle Ages there was unity in Europe such
as Europe had not known before or since, not even when the
legions of imperial Rome made Western Europe one and
Roman. High noon came in the twelfth and thirteenth
centuries, and the final apotheosis of medieval thought was
achieved in the *Summa* of St. Thomas Aquinas.

Certain thinking of St. Thomas Aquinas is worth consideration, even from the viewpoint of a subject so remote
from medieval scholasticism as American concepts of the
relationship of Church and State. The medieval king in
his coronation oath swore to defend the Church, to repress
injustice, and to enforce justice. But by that oath the king
entered, so to speak, into a compact with the people to
rule with certain ends in view and in accordance with specific principles. If the king abandons those ends and principles, says St. Thomas, the people are not bound by the

compact. St. Thomas goes so far as to say that it is the will of the people operating through the king that makes a law. St. Thomas Aquinas and John Locke are not so many leagues apart as might be supposed, nor is the political thought of St. Thomas entirely repugnant to that of the Declaration of Independence. Men can reach the same conclusion from dramatically separated starting points and by radically different routes. The conclusion St. Thomas reached is not a surprising one in a medieval churchman; a free people and a free Church are fairly natural corollaries. The point is worth stressing, because actually from the fourteenth century through the seventeenth the dominant trend in thinking about the relationship of Church and State was farther removed from the American concept than was the viewpoint of the thirteenth century.

Another point worth stressing is the fundamentally different concept of the State which obtained in the thirteenth century from the one which obtained even in the fifteenth. In the thirteenth century the State was an amorphous thing, more to be expressed in social, class-structural, even economic terms than in terms that are geographical. Except in England, and not completely there, the national state was a thing of the future. Thus the State was both very much smaller and very much larger than the modern national State. Its political unit might be a single city; its effective unit might be a social class or a profession practicing the length and breadth of Europe. The medieval state could expand and contract almost indefinitely to fill the void that called for filling. The Church, on the other hand, could neither expand nor contract. It could not expand, because it had been universal from the hour of its creation. It could not contract for the same reason. This is slightly esoteric in the telling but extremely practical in the application, since the physical boundaries of Church and State were never the same in the Middle Ages. Any comparison of thinking about Church and State in the Middle Ages and in the centuries after the fourteenth is utterly without foundation unless it takes into full consideration the entirely different concept of the State which obtained then and later. There is no lesson the Middle Ages have to teach more important than the first lesson of all. In that lesson we learn how different the Middle Ages were from the ages of the modern world.

THE FIRST SIGNS OF A MODERN WORLD

The first dim foreshadowing of the modern world began to appear in the fourteenth century. Councils inside the Church and outside it began to threaten the single, focal, final mountain peak of authority which the papacy had been a century before. At the highest secular level the power of kings increased; among the villeins and the artisans in the rural and urban lower depths there were uneasy stirrings and minor eruptions of revolt. The situation in France was typical of the first development. France and the king of France loomed larger than before in the real order of things; the Emperor, the Empire, and the whole hypothetical order dwindled by comparison. The French were becoming conscious of themselves as a race and a nation, and the autonomy of the king of France was set forth in pleas not to be ignored because they were unhistorical. Pope Boniface VIII warned Philip the Fair, "The arrogance should not arise in Gaul which proclaims that it recognizes no superior. The Gauls lie, because by right they are and ought to be under the King and Emperor of Rome." Philip had the confidence to answer, "Before there were priests the King of France had the rule of the kingdom and was able to make its laws."[3] John of Paris, in his *De Potestate*

Regia et Papali, analyzed the single universal society and found the concept valid only in the spiritual realm. He held that one universal faith is necessary, but not one universal sovereignty in things temporal. The diversity of mankind and the individuality of property demanded a temporal rule that was localized and diversified. Peter Dubois talked the calm, cold practicality of power politics. He held that whatever the theories and traditions, Philip the Fair had the temporal power and the Emperor and Pope did not. Let Philip assume full temporal authority; let the Pope save souls.

The last voice of the Middle Ages, in politics as in things more nearly permanent, is that of Dante. His *De Monarchia* is what Professor Dunning claims for it, "logically the most complete and perfect system that we have of imperialistic philosophy." But even in this last magnificent plea for the medieval concept, this plea for an earthly prince of peace whose sublime function it will be to realize on earth the mission of the Prince of Peace, the Hildebrandine thesis is reversed. Dante argues that monarchy, or empire, is the ideal form of world government, that the Roman people acquired the right of empire by the gift of God, and that the Emperor is as directly and as divinely chosen as the Pope. An epitaph and not a prophecy, such is Lord Bryce's verdict on *De Monarchia,* but there is in it something of prophecy as well. Dante pays full homage to the respect the Emperor owes the Pope, his fellow sovereign in another and a higher realm, but he also stresses the divine right of the Emperor. From the divine right of the Emperor to the divine right of kings is not an impossible step. As Bartolus of Sassoferrato puts it, "Each king in his kingdom is the emperor of his kingdom."

The facts of European life were tending toward the day when each king in his kingdom would be emperor of his

kingdom, and, as always, the philosopher appeared to give
the facts their justification. His name, while far from legion,
is not a single name. There appeared Marsiglio of Padua,
John of Jandun, Michael of Cesena, and William of Ockham.
Marsiglio of Padua (c.1275–c.1342) is not entirely representative of what is really more an anti-papal than a pro-
imperial group of thinkers, but his radicalism takes the form
that points directly toward the Reformation and so is most
pertinent to our theme. It is to be found in his *Defensor
Pacis*, presented to the Emperor Ludwig of Bavaria in 1324.

There is as much Aristotle in Marsiglio as in any scho-
lastic. Society arises from the nature of man, government
from the needs of society: "According to truth and the
opinion of Aristotle, the legislator . . . is the people, or a
majority of them . . . commanding or determining that
something be done or refrained from in the field of social
human action, under the pain of some temporal punishment."[4] Either the citizen-legislators act directly or through
delegates who are their agents. Their will is executed
through the *pars principans*, the executive organ of the
state. What form the executive should take is vague, but
Marsiglio makes it clear that an elective monarchy is prefer-
able to an hereditary one. The doctrine of popular sovereignty is carried over bodily and boldly into the Church.
The Church also is a society; sovereignty is vested in all
its members; the organ for expressing their authority is the
council, which must be representative in number and character (*in quantitate ac qualitate*, whatever the latter enigmatic word meant to Marsiglio). The laity as well as the
clergy should be represented in the council, which should
by majority vote interpret the Scriptures and legislate both
the spiritual and the temporal functioning of the Church.
But Marsiglio draws a crystal-clear distinction between the
sort of authority to be held by his temporal and spiritual

legislature. The former should have effective power, the latter only power of persuasion. The Church may teach man the road to salvation, but it may not force him down its path. As for the Pope, Marsiglio recognizes a certain historical pre-eminence in the bishop of Rome, but in every other sense puts him on a level with the other bishops.

The enormous fame of the *Defensor Pacis* in the twilight period between the Middle Ages and the Reformation depended almost entirely on the violent attack in it upon the Pope and the Church as then constituted. Modern interest tends to center in the first part, where Marsiglio presents his philosophy of society and the State. Its tone is startlingly modern, with its suggestions of Locke, Rousseau, and Thomas Jefferson. As a corrective, the reader should recall that its tone is also startlingly ancient, with it suggestions of Aristotle, Pericles, and the Greek city-state. What we actually see in Marsiglio is our first glimpse of the other side of the watershed. We have left the Middle Ages behind and entered the modern world, but Marsiglio is no inspired prophet of the eighteenth century to come. Rather there is in Marsiglio as well as in modern democracy much of the theory of the Roman Republic and the practice of the Greek city-state.

During the fourteenth and fifteenth centuries an impressive number of changes took place in both Church and State, and in the relationship of the two. Accepting the prophetic interpretation of the *Defensor Pacis*, we may say that the course of history followed the general directions which Marsiglio mapped out, although within these two hundred years political reality did not reach his theoretical conclusions. Adequate treatment of this series of changes is to be found in historical studies of impressive proportions; there is need here merely to name some of the more significant.

CENTURIES OF CONFUSION

In the Church there appeared dissident and heretical sects. It was the age of the Lollards and the Hussites, and orthodoxy's finger of suspicion might be pointed at the least likely persons, as Chaucer's Host points it at the Parson. Originally, the Lollards were members of the Alexian fraternity and cared for the poor and sick. Later the term was applied in England to the itinerant preachers, followers in the main of Wyclif, who opposed the organization of the Church, denied certain of its dogmas, and came to disaster after the Peasants' Revolt of 1381. By the Lollards, as by the sects in general, something that was in intent primitive and purified Christianity was preached and practiced. The contrast did exist between the simplicity, equality, poverty, and brotherhood of the early Church and the pomp and circumstance, the wealth, power, and ascending levels of hierarchical magnificence of the medieval Church. Men saw the contrast and began to denounce it. Carried into the secular realm and put in economic terms, that denunciation reached its climax in the socialism of the Taborites in Bohemia. "No mine and thine any more; private property is mortal sin."

These were the centuries of the papal exile in Avignon, of the Western Schism, of the rival popes and a nationalistic split in the support of rival papacies, the English and the Germans against the French. It was a time of confusion and discontent in the minds of honest men, a time when God-fearing men walked in spiritual twilight. It was the time when the councils strove for order in the Church, and some in the councils for supremacy in the Church. From the councils the papacy emerged supreme and unshaken, but never since has it had a temporal power like that of Hildebrand.

These were the centuries when the modern nations began to harden into form, when the medieval unity of Christendom crumbled, and revolt against the Church meant a gain of power for the State. At a time when the social order was churning from below yet hardening from above, when traditions were being challenged and then shattered, old and eternal verities no longer were accepted. Church and State were no longer viewed by all men as immutable instrumentalities of the will of God; an increasing number came to regard them as instrumentalities of the will of man, subject to change as man's advantage dictated, or seemed to dictate. When that frame of mind had been welded firm, Western Europe was ready for the Protestant Reformation.

2

The Reformation and Its Consequences

When the massive figure of Martin Luther appears and the titanic sequence of events he inaugurates, a word of warning must be said about perspective. In today's perspective it appears that the Reformation looked toward the future. In the perspective of its own day and from the viewpoint of that day, the Reformation looked squarely toward the past. Desiderius Erasmus and St. Thomas More belonged in spirit much more truly to the world of today than did Martin Luther and Philip Melanchthon. Erasmus and More looked hopefully, adventurously, with eager anticipation toward the future; Luther and Melanchthon looked earnestly, ardently, with burning conviction toward the past. The Reformation was not born of a determination to bring something new into the world; its purpose was to bring back something very old.

The spirit of Martin Luther, closely rooted in the soil of Germany which his peasant forebears had tilled, was conservative and tenacious. Luther's spirit did not burn with a desire for change; it smoldered with resentment at the

changes that had already occurred. Back to one book, Holy
Writ; back to one law, the law of God; back to one goal,
the life eternal; such is the essential message of his life
and writings. But precisely because there is so much of the
medieval mystic to the character and pronouncements of
Martin Luther, there stems from him a bewildering diversity
of beliefs and attitudes. Luther sought direct inspiration
from the Scriptures as the direct and literal word of God,
but he did not recognize this search as the personal right
of all men. He tended to undervalue the importance of the
Church and thus increase by natural compensation the
importance of the Prince. Democracy and the divine right
of kings, religious tolerance and religious persecution are
among the things implicit in the thought of Martin Luther.
George III is his ideological descendant, and so is Thomas
Jefferson; Cotton Mather looks back to Luther, and so does
Roger Williams. Hence arises the impossibility of reading
with assurance what partisans have written about the life,
thought, writings, and influence of Martin Luther. All tend
to be right in part and wrong in part. Out of Luther's
mysticism grew dogmas of Church and State, of God and
man, as plants grow in a rain forest. Nature is consistent
only to the principle of diversity. Great elemental human
forces like Martin Luther are the same.

The most important book for Luther, obviously, was the
Bible. Second, on his own testimony, was the work of St.
Augustine. Third was the fourteenth-century compendium
he published in 1516 under the title *Theologia Deutsch*.
Luther himself testifies that he learned more from it of
God, Christ, man, and all things than from any book save
the other two. A certain consistency runs through this compendium of medieval German mysticism; it may be found
most clearly expressed in the thought of Meister Eckhart
(1260–1327). Eckhart was a Dominican, high in his order,
as Henry Osborn Taylor puts it, a speculative spirit drawn

toward God as the ultimate, universal reality. The quest for God is the soul's true life; absorption by God is the soul's bliss and salvation. Grace is God's gift, to render more nearly perfect the soul of man. Granted the gift, the soul may understand and love; without the gift, the light to salvation is never lit. Luther read Eckhart and approved. Mysticism turns inward, German mysticism most sharply of all. Martin Luther's mysticism tends to obliterate all but God the Creator and Luther the created. Yet the temporal exists and must be reckoned with. For some of the journey the two lives are parallel, the life of the world and the life of eternity. Then the former ends and the latter abides.

LUTHER'S POLITICAL THOUGHT

Out of this mystical belief that before long, even as time is measured, only the will of God matters, grows that confused and vague body of beliefs that comprise, if anything comprises, Luther's political thought. It is best expressed in his *Von Weltlicher Uberkeyt,* which deals in the main with the divinely established limits of human authority. God is the Creator, man the created. Obedience in the only sense that carries a full and valid meaning is due to God. The Bible is God's message of salvation addressed to man. Implicit in a viewpoint that makes no proviso for authoritative interpretation is the principle that the message of Scriptures cannot be misunderstood. At that implicit principle is the great fork in the road: to the right lie Calvinism and the theocratic state, to the left lie democracy and religious tolerance.

What is the role of the State, in a universe where God speaks directly and in unmistakable terms to the soul of man? The State, obviously, is without responsibility and authority where belief and conscience are concerned. Nor

is the State a law-making agency in any sense that has a full
and cogent meaning. The law is of God and from God. It
binds man, including the civil magistrate. The State is a
law-enforcing agency, administering a law of God that
exists unchangeably from all eternity. In two places is that
law written, in Scripture and in the heart of man. Luther
is of the Middle Ages in dissociating entirely political authority and lawmaking power. By his logic, which is not the
logic of the modern world, tyranny and freedom can and
often do live side by side. Where Caesar is tyrannical, one
should bear the tyranny in a spirit of Christian resignation,
but one must not render to Caesar one jot or tittle of what
is God's. The oppressed subject is still the free Christian.

The practical test of Luther's thesis came in the Peasants'
War (1525–26). Strange fruit was budding on his tree of
mystical freedom, nor was it ever clear to him how the
branch could bear the fruit. At first he exhorted the peasants
to have recourse to prayer, reminding them that inequalities
were integral to the earthly plan and that in no sense did
they impair the Christian's spiritual liberty. But when violence followed, something elemental in Martin Luther
poured out like molten lava. In his *Against the Murderous
and Robbing Mobs of Peasants* he urged the princes to kill
the peasants without mercy; in his *Against the Heavenly
Prophets* he cried that "Herr Omnes" must be checked by
the sword and the law, as beasts by the bars of the cage.
Democracy is implicit in Luther, but so are many other
very different things.

Probably the final balance of Luther's influence was to
increase the power of the State against the freedom of the
one or the few. To Luther the law of God is one. Its message
is in Scripture and in the hearts of men. This message is the
law of God and the rule of salvation. The need for a State
arises from the fact that all men do not hear the word of
God in a spirit of obedience. The magistrate does not make

the law, which is of God, but enforces it. His realm is the temporal, and the proper ordering of it is his responsibility. Included in the proper ordering is the maintenance of churches where the word of God is truly preached and the truly Christian life is taught by precept and example. In his realm, subject to the law of God, the Prince is supreme, nor has man the right to rebel against him. But if the Prince contravenes the law of God, man may be passively disobedient, in obedience to a higher and the only finally valid law. The final effect of Luther's teaching was to lessen the power of the Church, and by way of natural corrective to increase the power of the State. It is vital to his thinking that since the Kingdom of God is spiritual, ecclesiastical power in the temporal realm is usurped; since the kingdoms of the earth are physical, the power of Princes in the temporal realm is natural and in accordance with the will of God. In the Prince, power; from the people, obedience; for the State, unity. As an objective for the Prince there is something very utilitarian in this orderly arrangement of mortal life, and Martin Luther gave it a moral sanction.

MELANCHTHON

Philip Melanchthon ranked next to Luther and Calvin in his influence on sixteenth-century Protestantism. The gentle, scholarly, benign Melanchthon did not have in his backbone the iron of Martin Luther nor the tungsten steel of John Calvin. He was an academician, far more sensitive than Luther, far less certain of himself, always facing the unhappy paradox which so often besets the intellectual. In the realm of reason his theological convictions made logic to him, but in the realm of life they made trouble for him. Melanchthon would follow a line of thought over the horizon, but it troubled him to follow a line of action out into the breakers.

As a political thinker, in an intellectual realm where thought is translated into action more directly than in some realms, his tendency was to evade difficulties. His political thought changed as time went on, swinging away from the quarter where democracy and religious toleration were to develop, into the quarter which was to harbor theocracy and religious intolerance. He believed government to be of divine institution, as part of the all-embracing design of God which includes a meeting of the needs of man. Thus government represents the will of God and the need, but not the will, of man. By corollary, obedience to government is a religious duty. Melanchthon drew no distinctions among the forms of government; all were instituted by God and all bear the marks of divine sanction. Rebellion against government in any form is rebellion against the will of God.

Thus far Melanchthon's thought follows the course of Luther's. He agrees with Luther that the rights of the Prince are limited by the law of God in its twofold revelation, Scripture and the human heart. But Melanchthon's concept of the natural law goes farther than Luther's. Melanchthon held that the right to property arose from the natural law and so is a sacred thing, and that the protection of property is one of the primary duties of the Prince. As early as Philip Melanchthon's *De Officio Principum* (1539) the nuptials between capitalism and Protestantism were being celebrated. Melanchthon went beyond Luther also in his concept of the relationship between the Prince and the Church. Luther held that the Prince's responsibility and power extended only to the maintenance of a Church where the word of God is truly preached; Melanchthon held that the primary purpose of government is to organize, cherish, and maintain the religious life of the community. Again, as early as Melanchthon's *De Officio Principum* the cast of Calvinism begins to take shape in the thinking of the reformers.

In Melanchthon, mind and heart were at variance where the treatment of heretics was concerned. In 1530 he was content to take a position very similar to the modern attitude toward political heterodoxy: if religious teaching implied or invited sedition, it could not be tolerated. By 1539 he had withdrawn from this intellectual salient; he then held that the Prince should uproot heresy by force. But when the mind had finished, the heart spoke. Catholicism, which Melanchthon deemed heretical by its additions to true faith, might be tolerated, but a heresy that blasphemed by denial must be crushed. This stand, hard to parallel in the clouded annals of theological debate, does credit to the heart, less credit to the head. Heresy is subtraction, not addition. Many a speculative thinker of Melanchthon's century could sift through that sieve.

The final balance of Melanchthon's influence, even more markedly than Luther's, is on the side of increased power for the State. For Melanchthon also, the Prince does not make the law, which is from God, but enforces it. The political power of the Prince is derived directly from God and not delegated by the people. Once one denies that obligation can be created by man, one has laid the foundation for the thesis of the divine right of kings, although Melanchthon did not dream of the structure of absolutism that would be raised on the foundations that he laid any more than did Luther. Melanchthon is as inconclusive as Luther in his political thinking, and thus his influence also radiates in contradictory directions. His concept of the responsibility of the Prince toward the Church points toward Calvin, and his concept of the responsibility of the Prince toward property points toward capitalism. His concept of natural and immovable limits to human authority points to Huguenot thinking and, far beyond the horizon, to the Declaration of Independence; his concept of that authority as derived from God and not delegated by man points to the divine rights of kings. This is contradictory and confusing, but strangely varying seeds of thought were germinating in the same seedbeds in sixteenth-century Germany.

THE ANABAPTISTS

None of the seeds were stranger and more nearly infinite in their potential variety than those which grew into that complex of always confusing and frequently contradictory beliefs called Anabaptism. To elucidate the theological maze in which ardent spirits and usually ignorant minds, visionaries, prophets, enthusiasts, and malcontents found themselves, happily lies far outside our purpose and is not essential to it. Yet some common denominator must be given to make the term Anabaptism intelligible. The obvious one is the most helpful: the great majority of those known as Anabaptists believed in the necessity for adult baptism as a prerequisite for reception into the Church. To complete the common denominator, one may add that the visionaries and prophets, the enthusiasts and malcontents generally believed in the direct inspiration from God which is known by many names, with "the inner light" the most easily recognized. Virtually all those known in the sixteenth century as Anabaptists believed in one or the other of these dogmas, and most of them believed in both.

Obviously nothing that remotely resembles a philosophy of the relationship between Church and State can emerge from the explicit thinking of people whose common denominators are a belief in adult baptism and in the inner light. But the Anabaptists were that sort of submerged and persecuted minority to whom the inner light gives the inner strength, and the logical consequences of the thinking of such people can be highly significant. Furthermore, the Anabaptists have endured; their direct descendants are the "plain people" of Pennsylvania, the Mennonites and the Amishmen.

Adult baptism is the key to the religious thought of the Anabaptists. Infant baptism implies that a child may be admitted into the Church without his understanding or personal consent. Such a church must be a formal organization, with sponsored membership possible for those whose years permit neither faith nor understanding. Adult baptism implies a different concept of the Church. The anabaptized are the elect of a visible church which is essentially a religious community of the elect. But obviously such a church could in no sense be a State Church. The Prince could neither bring it into being, regulate it, nor enforce membership in it; indeed, any connection between the State and such a church could only be injurious to the Church. Adult baptism on the surface is remote from the concept of a separated Church and State, yet such separation is implicit in the rationale of Anabaptism. The call to such a church can never come from the palace of the Prince; it must come from the Kingdom of Heaven, to those who have the inner light. (Sometimes across the deep gulf the centuries join hands. In 1947, Justice Jackson of the United States Supreme Court said of the American public school, "The assumption is that after the individual has been instructed in worldly wisdom he will be better fitted to choose his religion." The source of such thinking is not Protestantism in general, as Justice Jackson seemed to think. It is Anabaptism.)

Thus in the Germany of the early sixteenth century there were two currents flowing in the opposite directions beneath the broad surface of the Reformation. With the usual risks attendant on simplification, one may say that the major current is best observed in the thought of Luther and Melanchthon, the minor current in the thought of the Anabaptists. The major current was toward a State Church supported by the Prince, with membership a formal and even a required matter. Melanchthon goes farther than Luther in the direction of Calvin, but both point toward Calvin. The Anabaptists conceive of the Church as a body of the elect. Over such a body the Prince has neither responsibility nor authority, and interference by the Prince is quite certain to be harmful to it. The minor current is toward a church entirely separated from the State, with membership the result of direct election by God.

The logic of the Anabaptist position brought the believers into direct conflict with the civil authority and led to their persecution. From their view of the relationship between the Church and the Prince came the corollary, not surprising however hard to justify in logic, that government is in essence a repressive evil. The Prince is not God's lieutenant but God's foe. The Anabaptists rejected service to the Prince in every form, including the bearing of arms, the filling of civil office, the performing of the normal functions of citizens in a community. In effect they became religious anarchists, and as such were persecuted.

THEOCRACY IN MÜNSTER

In 1534 Anabaptist government was established in Münster. A theocracy was instituted under Jan Matthys, and apostles sallied forth to convert the world. The city was besieged by the Bishop of Münster, and Matthys was slain. Jan Beukels of Leyden succeeded him, and his daily revelations, which included a justification of polygamy, shocked the land. The city fell in 1535, and Anabaptism became once more what it had been before, an exclusively religious movement with its traditional attitude of quietism. In the

Netherlands it came under the directing influence of a former Catholic priest, Menno Simons (1492–1559), minister of the Anabaptists at Groningen. The Mennonites, as his followers came to be called, adopted the common doctrine of non-resistance, but continued to hold the Anabaptist position where bearing arms, taking oaths, and filling civil offices were concerned. Gradually the German-speaking Anabaptists came under the influence of Menno Simons. Stringent measures taken against the Anabaptists in Switzerland during the seventeenth century led to their virtual extermination there, but the wisdom and industry of Menno Simons bore fruit elsewhere in Germany and the Netherlands. In 1682 William Penn offered the Mennonites refuge and religious liberty, and the first society of Mennonites in the New World was organized in 1683 at Germantown, Pennsylvania. Today's tourists watching for the horse-drawn rigs and the untrimmed beards in the Pennsylvania Dutch country are really seeing the spiritual descendants of Jacob Amman and Menno Simons jealously guarding the faith of their fathers.

It may be difficult to deduce a political philosophy from the thinking of people who recognize one Kingdom only, a Kingdom not of this world. But certainly opposition to a State Church follows logically from the thinking behind adult baptism. Belief in the Church as a non-inclusive association follows logically from the belief that those form the Church to whom God has given the inner light. Opposition to the thesis of the divine right of kings follows logically from the denial that the Prince is God's lieutenant, or that God chooses to have a lieutenant. There is no more reason to believe that the Anabaptists were explicit believers in a separation of Church and State and in religious tolerance than that others of their century held such modern views, but the natural drift of their thinking was in that direction. The natural drift of Luther's thinking, and Melanchthon's, and above all Calvin's, was in the opposite direction.

JOHN CALVIN

As an influence on the relationship of Church and State in America, John Calvin transcends in importance the other continental reformers, individually and taken all together. That importance arises from two basic facts: Calvin was the only reformer to construct in fact as well as in theory a State, and Calvin's State was the model of the Massachusetts Bay Colony. By the significance of these facts is the importance of Calvin to be measured.

"Accusative Case," his fellow students at the College of Montaigu called him. Even as a youth he was bright and sharp, sedate and severe, and above all, censorious. He had been destined for the priesthood by his Catholic parents, and when he was twelve his father's employer, the bishop of Noyon, set aside for his education some of the revenue from the Chapel de la Gesine, in the Noyon cathedral. He received the tonsure in 1521, but soon he was treading roads that led far from Rome. He had his Latin in Paris at the College of La Marche and his dialectics at the College of Montaigu. Law came in 1527 and 1528 at the universities of Orléans and Bourges. At Bourges he sat before Andreas Alciati, then the law's brightest light in all Europe; of comparable significance was his friendship with the learned Melchior Wolman, who taught him Greek and the Gospel according to Martin Luther. In November 1533, he prepared for his friend the rector of the university, Nicholas Cop, a speech on the necessity for the reformation of the Church. The subsequent explosion blew him out of Paris. He found a friend in Margaret of Navarre, settled in Angoulême, and worked on his *Institutes,* returned to Paris in 1534, and found there was no place in Paris nor in France for John Calvin. He went to Strassburg, from there to Basel, and, in July 1536, found himself in Geneva. Calvin was predestined for Geneva, and Geneva for him.

Guillaume Farel, perfervid leader of the tiny evangelical group at Geneva, knew that in this wayfarer burned a flame hotter and brighter than his own. He induced Calvin to stay and become pastor of the flock. The rest belongs to what is, or should be, the familiar pre-history of the United States. At Geneva the Calvinistic Church-State was brought into being, one of the two states in all history brought into being by Protestantism as such. The other was modeled after Geneva and was built on the shores of Massachusetts Bay. In the history of Geneva and in the postulates of Calvin's *Institutes,* especially as presented in the definitive editions, the Latin of 1559 and the French of 1560, may be observed in practice and in theory the most important exposition of the relationship of Church and State that the sixteenth century produced. It is an exposition of unrivaled importance in the historic approach to the study of that relationship in the United States.

Calvinistic theology starts with an axiom: the Bible is the self-evident Word of God. Its authority is internal, depends on the interpretation of no church, and requires no defense. The *Institutes of the Christian Religion* is the key to its essential teaching, but it is essential to Calvin's concept that in the real sense no key is necessary. God made the world, and its end and purpose is the greater glory of God. God predestined men to heaven or hell; the saved glorify God's mercy, the damned glorify God's justice. It is customary to say that Calvin denied the freedom of the human will. As a matter of literal fact, this is not true. Calvin strove to avoid the position by the doctrine of efficacious grace, the mark of God's free and absolute mercy by which the elect are saved. Others are not saved because they have the wills of fallen beings, wills necessitated toward evil. To few persons today does the distinction seem to connote a difference. Calvin may not have denied the freedom of the human will, but the logic of Calvin's theology did.

THE VISIBLE AND INVISIBLE CHURCH

That logic further dictates that there is an invisible Church as well as a visible one. The members of the first are known only to God; they are the elect. But this invisible Church needed its visible counterpart, and Calvin believed, as firmly as did the Catholics, that there is only one true, universal Church. It was his lifework, not to bring this Church into being, since it already existed, but to restore it to what he deemed the purity of its original being, to restore the early Christian community as the New Testament describes it. In strict logic there can be no hierarchical grades in the invisible Church; who can measure God's efficacious grace as meted out to the elect? But the Church visible and the Church invisible are not one and the same, and in the Church visible hierarchical grades are necessary. Hence the pastors who preached the Word, gave the sacraments, and preserved discipline at Geneva. They were the clerical officers of the first grade. They were aided by officers of the second grade, the elders or lay presbyters, in governing the Church. To the officers of the third grade, the deacons, were assigned the Church's works of corporal mercy, the care of the poor and the sick. In theory the pastors were appointed by a council elected annually; in effect they were a small, self-electing group. By 1555 supreme power in Geneva was vested in the self-perpetuating council of pastors and in the consistory, which was representative of the Church as a whole but was pastor-controlled.

To pass from the fact of the Calvinistic Church-State to the theory involves one in no serious contradictions. Calvin had the French logic and the French willingness to act; what he believed in theory, he did in Geneva. For much of the way his political theory parallels that of Luther and Melanchthon. The State was the product of the will of God and the need of man. The Prince is God's lieutenant on earth, and the duty to honor and obey him is absolute. Rebellion against the Prince is rebellion against God, and it is no less rebellion if the Prince's rule is unjust and contrary to the will of God. This is true because the Prince holds his grant of power, not from man but from God, and how he administers that power is his personal and direct responsibility to his Maker. If obedience to the Prince means disobedience to the law of God, the higher law prevails and disobedience to the Prince becomes a moral imperative. But this means passive disobedience only and in no sense countenances rebellion. For man to rebel against the Prince is for man to abrogate the right of God to choose, and later to judge, His lieutenant, and that is sacrilege. On this point, if on little else, Protestants and Catholics of the sixteenth century agreed. So important did Calvin deem the distinction between passive and active disobedience that he devoted to the Anabaptists a large part of the chapter in the *Institutes* which treats of civil government.

In the 1541 edition of the *Institutes* he listed the purposes for which the State exists: ". . . that idolatry, blasphemy of the name of God and against His truth and other scandals to religion, be not publicly set forth and broadcast among the people; that public peace be not troubled, that each be secured in what is his own, that men's intercourse may be without fraud and violence, in fine that among Christians there be some public and visible form of religion and that humanity be settled among men."[1]

The State must suppress idolatry, blasphemy, and other scandals to religion. Put in positive terms the corollary, as in Luther, is that the State must maintain churches where the word of God is truly preached and the truly Christian life taught by precept and example. Church and State must work in harmony to insure that "there may be some public and visible form of religion and that humanity be settled among men." But in the last analysis only the Church is competent to declare what is the godly life. The Church is by nature the senior partner in the Calvinistic order, with a constant tendency to absorb entirely its lesser confrere. Calvin inherited a governmental framework at Geneva, and the Geneva Church remained part of that framework. But when Calvin's work was in its final stages by 1555, the part had absorbed the whole. The council of pastors and the consistory representing the Church as a whole, both Calvin's creations, had the real power in Geneva. Calvin had done more than bring into being a State Church. He had created a Church-State.

Calvin's concept of the Church is of fundamental importance. It is an audacious concept, finely imaginative, and it cuts with one slashing stroke the Gordian knot of church organization: "Wherever we see that the word of God is preached in its purity and listened to, and the sacraments administered as instituted by Christ, there can be no doubt that there is the Church. . . . The universal Church is the multitude of men who heed the truth of God and the doctrine of His words, however diversified they be in nation. . . . In this universal Church the churches distributed in each town and village are so comprised that each has the title of The Church and its authority."[2]

Let us start again with the axiom of Calvinism: the Bible is the self-evident word of God. Its authority is internal, depends on the interpretation of no church, and requires no defense. There is but one possible correct interpretation of the word of God, and it is the only interpretation possible for an honest man of sound intelligence to reach. It would be contrary to the justice of God for His self-evident word to admit of more than one sincere interpretation. Where the word is truly preached and the sacraments properly administered, there is the Church. The Church is one and it is manifold. Every local church that preaches the true word has the title and authority of the universal Church. The Church is in Geneva. Later it will be in Scotland. Still later it will be in Boston. It may be in lands of which John Calvin has never heard, and the true word be preached in tongues of which he and the pastors of Geneva have no understanding. Whether one accepts or rejects the concept, it is an audacious and finely imaginative one.

THE SEEDS OF DEMOCRACY

Furthermore, it is a masterful one in the political sense. As time passed, the influence of Calvin spread beyond Switzerland and France, through the Netherlands and parts of Germany, across the Channel to England and Scotland. Calvin was fighting a desperate fight against the disintegrating tendency evident from the start in Protestantism. Only a coherent body of dogma universally accepted by the Protestant congregations and taught in the atmosphere of a church-controlled State could stay that tendency. In 1548 Calvin wrote to Protector Somerset, "The Church of God will never save itself without a catechism." Nothing less than the creation of a Protestant Church in world-wide opposition to the Catholic Church was the goal of John Calvin. He failed, but the thunder of his failure echoes to the present day. John Calvin was one of the great makers of the modern world.

The seeds of democracy were present in Calvinism from the start. Some of them were seeds planted by Calvin himself, in other and more important respects they were seeds sowed by the Calvinistic churches in their process of development. Calvin was of his age in denying to individuals the right of rebellion against the wicked Prince. But Calvin drew a distinction in this regard between the individual and the minor magistrates who comprised the Estates-General. They represented constitutional order, and when the public welfare demanded resistance to the wicked Prince, they had the moral right to offer it. Beyond this, Calvin weighs in the *Institutes* the relative merits of the basic forms of government, monarchy, aristocracy, and democracy. He finds that each has its inherent virtues and each its characteristic vices. "Liberty with becoming moderation" is the phrase he applies to ideal government, and he finds it an ideal most likely to be realized in that mixed form of government God ordained for the children of Israel.[3] "He established an aristocracy bordering on popular government among the Israelites, keeping them under that as the best form, until he exhibited an image of the Messiah in David."[4] The superiority of the aristocratic republic to both the monarchy and the democracy is a Calvinistic fundamental.

The history of the local churches that accepted Calvinism shows a development of this concept which is logical, if not indeed inevitable, in the nature of their development. It was of the essence of Calvinism that the Church was manifold as well as one. Every local church that preached the true word had, in his view, the title and authority of the universal Church. But the local churches that accepted Calvinism were in a minority all over Europe. They were self-contained for reasons external as well as internal, and they had to live without the help and despite the hindrance of the State.

The democratic election of pastors, only a theoretical proviso in Geneva, became an actual procedure elsewhere. The stronger Calvinism grew in numbers, the stronger it grew politically. The time came here and there, at different times in different places, when Calvinistic or modified Calvinistic concepts of the State held sway. From the election of the pastor by a democratic process to the similar election of the civil magistrate was a natural step. The most dramatic instance came in Provincetown harbor the night before the Pilgrims first set foot on American soil, the night that the Mayflower Compact was signed.

But there was a deeper sense in which Calvinism, as it was worked out, promoted democracy. It was the universal sixteenth-century viewpoint that the Prince was the lieutenant of God and that when one obeyed the Prince, he obeyed one clause of the law of God. It was a next-to-universal sixteenth-century viewpoint that when the dictate of the Prince transgressed the law of God, the subject had a moral right to no more than passive disobedience. But passive disobedience in such a case was a moral imperative. Human nature, however, does not rest content with moral imperatives that are passive. Where there is an emotional will there is an ideological way, and before long the inheritors of Calvinism added the right of rebellion against the wicked Prince to their spiritual arsenal. There is no necessary connection between political democracy and the right to rebellion, but there is a historical connection. The United States of America was born when that right was exercised, and none exercised it with greater enthusiasm than the Calvinists of Boston.

John Knox against the Wicked Prince

The inheritor of Calvinism who added to his arsenal with the most dramatic and lasting effect the right of rebellion against the wicked Prince was John Knox. The wicked Prince was Mary Queen of Scots, one whose wickedness was lodged in the minds of her adversaries. She was a girl of nineteen, young, inexperienced, and frightened, a daughter of the Renaissance in a strange and dour land, when Knox defied her to her face. It was Knox's open defiance that prevailed among Calvinists after 1560, not the passive disobedience of Calvin, and the difference was portentous to Princes.

Knox started with the axiom expressed in his *The First Blast of the Trumpet Against the Monstrous Regiment of Women* (1558) that no woman can lawfully succeed to the throne. His immediate target was Mary Tudor, and her crime was Catholicism, as was the crime of the Queen of Scots. His conclusion was a duty "as well of the Estates as of the People . . . to remove from honour and authority that monster in nature."[5] Within a year Knox had advanced his salient against the wicked Prince. In his *Appellation* of 1558, written a year after *The First Blast* but published the same year, he issued to the people of Scotland an explicit appeal for revolt, declaring that to rebel against an idolatrous sovereign was the duty of a Christian people. "It is no less blasphemy to say that God hath commanded Kings to be obeyed when they command iniquity, than to say that God by his precept is author and maintainer of all iniquity."[6] "The punishment of such crimes as are idolatry, blasphemy and others that touch the Majesty of God, doth not appertain to kings and chief rulers only, but also to the whole body of that people, and to every member of the same, according to the vocation of every man and according to that possibility and occasion which God doth minister to revenge the injury done against his glory, what time that impiety is manifestly known."[7]

The context makes it clear that for idolatry and blasphemy is to be read Catholicism. Less reliable is the surface reading that Knox is advocating assassination. Later he explained his position by stating that the duty of killing the idolatrous king rested on "the people assembled together in one body of one Commonwealth.[8] Who was to judge what was idolatry and blasphemy? As always, we return to the crux of Calvinism: there is only one possible sincere interpretation of the Scriptures.

The famous interview with Mary Queen of Scots took place in 1561. The record is that of Knox, in his *History of the Reformation*. There is no reason to doubt the accuracy of the record. The speeches of Knox are the grave speeches of a major prophet of woe; the speeches of the Queen are those of a brave, frightened girl.

"God craves of Kings that they be as it were foster-fathers to his Church and commands Queens to be nurses unto his people."

"Yes (quoth she) but ye are not the Kirk that I will nourish. I will defend the Kirk of Rome for, I think, it is the true Kirk of God."

"Your will, madam, is no reason."

She replied that it was not her will but her conscience and study that brought her to this conviction. Knox dismissed her conscience as dependent on right knowledge, of which she had none, and her study as under false and biased teachers. And then she asked him the question that Calvinism never answered.

"Ye interpret the Scripture in one manner and they interpret in another. Whom shall I believe? And who shall be judge?"

"Ye shall believe God . . . there can remain no doubt but unto such as obstinately remain ignorant."

The interview ended. It had been a clash of minds so remote from each other that no clash took place. Knox could not understand the girl-queen nor is there any reason to believe that Mary could understand John Knox. No greater gulf ever opened in human ideologies than the gulf between the Renaissance and Calvinism, and it separated Knox and Mary.

Knox added the one conviction at which the legalistic mind of Calvin quailed. The Bible is the self-evident word of God. The Prince has the solemn duty direct from God to provide that the word of God be truly preached and practiced. If the Prince does not perform that duty, said Calvin, the people have the duty passively to disobey him. If the Prince does not perform that duty, said Knox, the people have the duty to put him to the sword of vengeance. In Calvinism the Church is the State, but in Knox far more than in Calvin the State and the Church both are the People. In neither man is there the faintest glimmer that even suggests to the backward-looking eye the distant dawn of tolerance. But in Knox the sword of the Almighty's vengeance in the hands of an outraged People is the first strange symbol of what some day will be democracy.

3

The Reformation Reaches America

There is a difference, which grows in significance the more one contemplates it, between the Reformation in England and on the Continent, and even in Scotland. Where the rest of Europe is concerned, one thinks of the Reformation primarily in terms of the Reformers, in terms of Luther, Melanchthon, the Anabaptists, Calvin, Knox, and the others. Where England is concerned, one thinks primarily in terms of the rulers, in terms of Henry VIII, Elizabeth, and James I. Viewed from the vantage point of four hundred years, the continental Princes are dwarfed by the Reformers; from the same vantage point the English Reformers are dwarfed by the Princes. The difference is one of the utmost significance, and it is never more significant than when it ceases to apply. It ceases to apply when one reaches the Puritans.

At the very dawn of the English Reformation, the Catholic position was expressed simply and directly by St. Thomas More in his *A Dialogue concerning heresyes and matters of religion*. "Is it (the Church) not this company and congregation of all those nations that . . . profess the name and faith of Christ? By this Church we know the Scripture and this is the very Church; and this hath begun at Christ and hath had him for their head and St. Peter, his vicar, after him and head under him and always since, and successors of his continually; and have had his holy faith and his blessed sacraments and his holy scriptures delivered, kept and conserved therein by God and his Holy Spirit." From this tree, in his viewpoint which has always been the Roman Catholic view, all other branches of Christianity are branches fallen. "We know evermore that the heretics be they that be severed and the Church the stock that they all came out of."[1]

This is the essentially historical belief that the Protestant sovereigns of England had to overthrow. Changes in doctrine will follow in due course at the hands of the Reformers, but the changes in doctrine will be secondary in importance as well as in time. Such was not really the case on the Continent, where the Reformation from the start was an effort to return the Church itself to the doctrines and practices of its apostolic days. The problem of Henry VIII was to wean the Church in England away from the Pope, but otherwise to leave it as little changed as possible.

To proclaim that the power of the Pope had ended in England was not enough. Consider the power ended; a vacuum is created. What will fill the vacuum constitutes the resulting problem. The clergy in point of fact have jurisdiction and authority. From whom do their powers come? The answer of the Catholics must be rejected by Henry. The vacuum created by the removal of the Pope can be filled only by the King. Henry must be vicar of Christ for England, and the visible head of the Church in England.

THE CHURCH OF ENGLAND

The process of reasoning used by the English Reformers to buttress Henry's claims proceeds logically enough, if one accepts its axioms. Christ founded a visible church. The Pope and the clergy do not have the right to govern it. But someone must have the right to govern it, since the alternative is chaos. Therefore the right to govern it must be secular. But if this is so, Christ must have instituted a secular control of the Church which later was usurped by the clerics. The record of such secular control, and the injunction to observe it, must be found in Scriptures. Knowing what must be found, the Reformers found the former in the Old Testament and the latter in St. Paul. Thus Henry, in becoming Head of the Church in England, is merely assuming his God-appointed right and performing his God-indicated duty. The relationship between Church and State in the England of Henry VIII finally is as clear-cut as the relationship in the Geneva of Calvin, and precisely the opposite. In Geneva the State will be an aspect of the Church; in England under Henry VIII the Church is an aspect of the State. Calvin will create the Church-State; Henry created the State Church.

But the latter phrase brings in another consideration. The Church in England means one thing, the Church of England something quite different. Henry's view of the Church is similar to Calvin's concept of the universal Church, but not entirely the same. To Calvin, as has been seen, the universal Church is real but invisible; where the word is truly preached and the sacraments properly administered, there is the true Church. Held together by invisible bonds that gird the world, these congregations where truth prevails comprise the universal Church. Henry's viewpoint appears officially in *A Necessary Doctrine and Erudition for any Christen Man* (1543): The universal Church comprises a group of localized churches united in true Christian belief and profession but each governed by the local secular ruler. "As they be distinct in places, so they have distinct ministers and divers heads in earth . . . yet be all these holy churches but one holy church catholic."

Thus Henry would have been satisfied with a Church in England and himself its head. But experience soon proved what logic indicated: to answer the question of sovereignty answers nothing, since it leaves unanswered the questions of religious belief. Henry soon sighted the same hard rock around which the Calvinists had to make their difficult and perilous way. If there is no one in the Church to interpret the Word of God with final authority, who is to do it? The Calvinistic answer we have seen: the meaning of the Word of God is clear to a sincere man of normal intelligence. Henry was an intelligent man, and he knew the deeper implications of the question. He avoided the question as long as he could, retaining everything he could of Catholicism except the authority of the Pope. But in his speech to Parliament in 1545 he had to face up to the issue. "If you know surely that a bishop or preacher erreth or teacheth perverse doctrine, come and declare it to some of our council or to us, to whom is committed by God the high authority to reform and order such causes and behaviours."[2] When a king assumes that position, and the final logic of Henry's position made it finally inevitable, a State Church has come into being. Henry is the final authority on Church doctrine and practice; the Church in England has become the Church of England, the Church has become an aspect of the State, and Henry has created the State Church.

QUEEN ELIZABETH

Elizabeth moved as slowly and reluctantly as her father in the direction that logic indicated. Her reasons are not far to seek; like her father, she was vastly more interested in the State than in the Church, and the lessons of the reigns of Edward VI and Mary did not escape her astute and practical intelligence. She inherited a realm where Catholicism was a factor, although a decreasing one, and where Puritanism was a factor and increasing. She inherited a position that was imperiled by a union between France and Scotland, motivated by the desire to supplant her on the throne with Mary Queen of Scots who was, in the Catholic view, the lawful heiress. The Calvinistic Lords of the Congregation, aided by a strange and only implicit alliance between Elizabeth and John Knox, established the Presbyterian Church in Scotland in 1560. But Elizabeth was too farsighted to imagine for a moment that strange alliances are lasting ones, too understanding of the ways of men to imagine that the Presbyterian spirit would brook the supremacy of the State over the Church. Across the Channel she had the object lesson of a France torn for decades by a grim religious war that was settled in 1598 by the Edict of Nantes, an edict spoken by the voice of exhaustion. She saw in the Netherlands a struggle that was partly a national war for freedom but also in large measure a religious war leveling in smoking ruins what had been the richest part of northern Europe. Had she lived longer, she might have seen in its early years the worst religious war in all European history begin to rack Germany, to make the land a mass of ruins, and to decimate the German people. It was with the best of good reasons that Elizabeth moved as slowly and reluctantly as her father in the direction that logic dictated.

One fact aided her mightily. The mass of the English people had no stomach for a war of the creeds. The instinct of the average Englishman was to regard religion as a matter for the State to settle. England had its enthusiasts who would turn to fire and the sword, but not nearly so many as had France, Germany, the Netherlands, or Scotland. The English, then as always, had the genius for compromise.

Consequently, Elizabeth moved with circumspect caution. Her major steps were three in number, the Act of Supremacy and the Act of Uniformity, both dating to 1559, and the gradual passage of the Thirty-Nine Articles in 1552–71. The one major step inevitable from the logic of her position was taken: she renewed the royal supremacy and thus declared her independence of Rome. But her terminology was more discreet than that of Henry. He had been "Supreme Head of the Church." She was "Supreme Governor of this Realm as well in all Spiritual or Ecclesiastical things or causes as Temporal." Words, carefully chosen and in sufficient volume, can often soothe. Furthermore, uniformity did not mean to her, as it did to her father, internal unity of faith but external unity of worship. A small fine was imposed if one did not go to church. If one did, one listened to a soothing, common-denominator sort of preaching. Most Englishmen, perhaps, were glad to be rid of enthusiasm. As Professor Hearnshaw puts it, "They willingly went to church and there composed themselves to sleep, thus gaining refreshment and vigour for the secular enterprises on which their hearts were set."

The day of reckoning, of course, was not permanently averted, although it was averted long enough to permit the day of Elizabeth. Certain tenets of the more devout were not standing the test of time. Royal supremacy was not visibly forwarding the development of the Christian Commonwealth; indeed, it was increasingly evident that the

Queen was using responsibilities and powers granted her by the Kingdom of Heaven to consolidate the kingdom of England. The general reading of the Scriptures was not producing that general doctrinal agreement among men of good will which was an axiom of Calvinism. The entire trend in the Church indicated that the court of last appeal in matters of dogma or ritual was the Queen, or the Queen in Parliament, and that the bishops held their authority, as Professor Allen puts it, "by virtue of a royal commission and for no other reason, exactly as do justices of the peace." By the last decade of the sixteenth century the Puritan restiveness was mounting to dangerous proportions, and Elizabeth was not one to tolerate the existence of unnecessary danger. The lesser voice of Whitgift had spoken and the greater voice of Hooker now spoke in answer to the Puritans. But the Queen acted. Her action was not a whit less drastic toward those who did not recognize her position under the Act of Supremacy and meet the simple requirements of the Act of Uniformity than was the action of her father or her sister.

The basic viewpoint of Elizabeth toward the relationship of Church and State must not be disguised by the cautious leniency of her general practice. She accepted fully her father's view that a national church had the right to decide its own doctrines, forms of divine service, and ecclesiastical organization. Gradually such Catholic doctrines as transubstantiation, the communion of saints, and purgatory were abandoned. The Mass was labeled a "blasphemous fable and dangerous deceit" (Articles of Religion, XXXI). But ecclesiastical organization remained unchanged in the main, and episcopacy was its principle. Beyond this there was relatively little of an affirmative nature in the Elizabethan settlement. There was no integrated theology, no established form of ritual, little of what normally comprises a church except the fact that it unquestionably had a head. The reason, of course, is to be found in Elizabeth's unwavering determination to keep the enthusiasts subdued. She wanted a church where the Anglo-Catholics and the Anglo-Calvinists could worship under the same steeple. She wanted it, not because she wanted a united church but because she wanted a united State. She viewed the Church as part of the State, and in the last analysis the sovereign and Parliament were, under Elizabeth, the intrepreters of Scriptures. The mantle of infallibility had not been discarded; it had been transferred to other shoulders, and it was worn, not in the interests of a true church but in the interests of a peaceful State. Not without reason do we think of the Reformation on the Continent and in Scotland primarily in terms of the Reformers, but in England primarily in terms of the rulers.

The point is of fundamental importance to the historical relationship of Church and State in the United States. Somewhere in religion there must be an ultimate fountainhead of authority. On the Continent the final, logical conclusion of the thought of Luther, Melanchthon, and Calvin was reached at Geneva, where the Church absorbed the State and the Church-State came into being. That is the tradition which the Puritans of England and later of New England inherited. In England the final, logical conclusion of the thought of Henry VIII, Elizabeth, and James I was reached at the royal court, where the State absorbed the Church and the State Church came into being. That tradition ultimately produced the Anglo-Catholicism of England, which later was transferred to the southern colonies.

The two viewpoints were completely irreconcilable. The diplomacy of Elizabeth was able to postpone the day, but the day of decision was certain to come. In England it came on the field of battle. In England no more than in France, the Netherlands, or Germany, was the battle won by either side. Ultimately the Established Church and the dissenters learned to live side by side on the principles of religious toleration and a respect for the individual conscience. In the United States it came more happily in the first article of the Bill of Rights, which provides that "Congress shall make no law respecting an establishment of religion, or prohibiting the free exercise thereof." The first Congress ruled out both the State Church and the Church-State, to the great and lasting benefit of the American people. Its action was not dictated by the spirit of secularism, nor did it result in the spirit of secularism. Secularism was almost, although not quite, as unimaginable at the end of the eighteenth century as it had been at the end of the sixteenth. To establish this fact, however, we must shift our primary focus from England to the colonies, and particularly to the sands of Plymouth and the shores of Massachusetts Bay.

THE PURITANS IN ENGLAND

Before we can reach Plymouth or the shores of Massachusetts Bay we must consider the prior position of the Puritans and the Puritan attitude toward the Church and State as they existed in England. The ultimate position of Puritanism at Boston in the glory of its high noon is the same as that of Calvinism at Geneva. The intermediate position of Puritanism in England, as its sun was rising behind a clouded sky, was something quite different.

Naturally there was little reaction within Protestant ranks under Henry VIII comparable to the later Puritan stirring under Elizabeth and James I. The victory was too recent and too uncertain to admit of that. But even under Henry there was an uneasy feeling among such sincere Protestants as Henry Brincklow[3] and Anthony Gilby[4] that a state of affairs which found a secular Prince replacing the Pope as head of the Church in England was not necessarily and finally a change for the better. Gilby was one of the group of religious refugees at Frankfort that must be called, if anything specific can be so called, the seedbed of English Puritanism.

Under Elizabeth these same persons, not yet in any sense except a partial and intellectual one dissenters, continued to rebel against the concept of a Parliament that was infallible in matters of religion. Fuel was heaped upon an already smoldering fire by the Vestiarian controversy. The surplice might be merely an ecclesiastical garment and, to the more placid members of the Church, a thing indifferent. To the dissenters it was a popish relic consecrated to idolatry. The marriage ring, the feast day, the organ, and many other instrumentalities and forms of worship soon joined the surplice in disfavor. If the Queen in Parliament ordained that they be used, the sovereign was ordaining the use of idolatrous rites and relics, and was contravening the law of God. The proto-Puritans accepted, as it were by instinct, the precepts from which developed in one direction the thinking of St. Thomas Aquinas and in another the thinking of John Calvin. The sovereign could not ordain what was contrary to the law of God; the concept of absolute power in the sovereign was one beyond their grasp. But they were not yet ready to go so far down the road even as Calvin went with his doctrine of passive disobedience, to say nothing of the more radical position of John Knox who would depose and even kill an idolatrous king. The proto-Puritans remained with the Church, sadly shaking their heads and praying for the day of enlightenment.

By 1579 Thomas Cartwright and Walter Travers were ready to make explicit their denial of Elizabeth's supremacy over the Church. Two *Admonitions to Parliament* were speedily issued, and those who had been dissenters before in a vague and personal way now had a cause with which they could align themselves. The next decade found their numbers growing steadily. Their influence began to penetrate Parliament, and by 1585 there was a Presbyterian party in England. The first Marprelate tract appeared in 1588, and by 1590 Elizabeth was taking action. It was as drastic and as bloody as anything done by her three predecessors.

Puritanism crushed to earth also rises again, and where it can rise to its full stature, as in Geneva and Boston, it takes the form of the Church-State. The Puritans of England conceived of the Church in national terms. They further conceived of it as self-governed and as necessarily distinct from a State whose sovereign did not accept the Puritan position. It is perhaps a helpful although in some ways an inaccurate simplification to say that they conceived of it as possessing true members, the godly who accepted the Puritan concepts, and excommunicate members, the ungodly who did not. Obviously the Church must be ruled by the godly, and the separation of Church and State was to insure that the ungodly, so numerous and so strong in the latter, might have no voice in running the Church. But that is a far different thing from saying that they favored separation of Church and State with the thought of tolerating the beliefs and practices of those who disagreed with them in both. The State, in their view, had the duty to maintain the true Church, but the State was in every sense subordinate to the Church. Had Calvinism been as strong in England as it was in Scotland, undoubtedly the English Puritans would have taken the full position assumed by Knox, and Elizabeth would have had to face a bearded English prophet of woe, just as Mary Queen of Scots faced a Scottish one. But Elizabeth was far more potent than Mary, and England quite another land from Scotland. The Puritans did not take the logical final position because they could not take it.

By 1585 there was a Presbyterian party in England, but by the same year there was a serious rift in Puritan ranks. Associated with the name of Robert Brown, those who dissented from dissent were variously known at various times as Brownists, Independents, and Congregationalists. Cartwright and Travers had insisted that ministers be elected by the members of the Church. Brown, a pupil of Cartwright, went one step farther. He denied to the magistrate all authority of an ecclesiastical nature. To him a church consisted of "true Christians united into a company, a number of believers who place themselves under the government of God and Christ."[5] In such a church all the members were kings and priests, the association was voluntary, and it was independent of every other association. Democracy was of its essence and its relationship to the Anabaptist position is self-evident. It is equally self-evident that to argue that a magistrate can bring such a church into being or can maintain it is sheer nonsense. "The church planted or gathered is a company or number of Christians or believers which, by a willing covenant made with their God are under the government of God and Christ, and keep his laws in one holy communion."[6] The Brownists parted company from the Anabaptists chiefly in not insisting on adult baptism and in not regarding civil government as necessarily evil. They remained in the company of the Presbyterians to the extent that they believed the magistrate had the duty to suppress false religion. Thus, in their view the position of the magistrate was one of negative but not positive power toward religion. He had the power and duty to suppress false churches, not the power and duty to bring into being the true Church. As for the identity of the true Church, as always in Calvinism the truth is self-evident to the man of normal intelligence and good will. The Brownists wanted religious toleration for themselves. That religious toleration for others was a logical deduction from their views was none of their planning. When this point is reached, it is possible to think in terms of Plymouth and Massachusetts Bay. From the Brownists stemmed the Pilgrims of

Plymouth, from the Presbyterians the Puritans of Boston. Both colonies stemmed, by reaction, from James I and the theory of the divine right of kings.

When Elizabeth died, the Puritans expected to come into their own. They pinned their hopes on the early training of her successor. James was born at Edinburgh on June 19, 1566. In July 1567 he became titular king, and John Knox preached his coronation sermon. At the age of four he was turned over to George Buchanan and a group of tutors assembled by him to be trained for the high office which the Kirk held in custody for him. James was to be the ideal Protestant Prince; Buchanan and his staff expended their finest efforts to this end, and the intellectual powers of Buchanan were of a high order. They made him one of the most tremendous pedants in the history of all the crowns of Europe, but they failed with abysmal totality in their primary aim. James not only rejected the concept of a sovereign submissive to the purposes of a Calvinistic Church-State; he became the embodiment in flesh and blood of the divine right of kings thesis. He got his book learning from Buchanan, but his ideas from the court of Henry III of France and probably from the *Republic* of Jean Bodin. By 1584 James had induced the Scottish Parliament formally to condemn the writings of Buchanan and had made it his undeviating policy to establish an episcopacy in Scotland and to re-establish monarchical control of the Church. His concepts are expressed in his *Basilikon Doron* (1598) and *The Trew Law of Free Monarchies* (1598). The Puritans of England soon were to see what their Scottish counterparts were viewing with dismay, that James was far more belligerently opposed to the Calvinistic Church-State than even Elizabeth had been. The reign of James in England was far from a period of unalloyed serenity for a Scot who never really understood the English and their institutions, but there was even less serenity for the Puritans under a monarch who understood thoroughly and accepted fully Jean Bodin's theory of sovereignty. James's determination toward the Puritans was to make them conform or to harry them out of the land. Legend has it that in 1608 he harried out of the land and into Holland a small band of Independents whose minister was John Robinson, whose ruling elder was William Brewster, and whose center was the town of Scrooby in Nottinghamshire. Dissatisfied with life in the Low Countries, in 1620 they hired the *Mayflower* and on November 11, old style, they entered Provincetown harbor. Before they landed at the tip of Cape Cod, they drew up the first written constitution in the world. A month later, after exploring the coast, they landed at Plymouth Rock.

4

The Church-States of Plymouth and Boston

It is essential for a clear understanding of what the Pilgrims meant to America to understand what the Pilgrims meant to Protestantism. The Pilgrims started in absolute obscurity. They were not "harried from the land," by James or by anyone else. There isn't a vestige of positive proof that the authorities in London were so much as aware of the existence of the little church at Scrooby, in Nottinghamshire. Yet this tiny and utterly insignificant band was the leaven that helped to form the final structure of Puritanism in New England. The Pilgrims have their obvious place of importance in American history in terms of their date of settlement. They have as well that far more pervasive importance, which has not entirely passed into history, that arose from their pattern of thinking about Church and State in Massachusetts.

The Pilgrims were the extreme leftists of the Reformation when they formed their church at Scrooby. They believed that the Reformation had not gone far enough, that the Reformers had assumed an infallibility no more palatable

when lodged in a ruler than when lodged in the Pope, that
the Church of England had rejected the Pope but not
Popery, that the bishops of the Church of England had no
more authority than the bishops of the Church of Rome. In
the autumn of 1608 they left the Church of England and
formed a church of their own. Nowhere else in England was
there a true church. To them the Church of England was a
mockery of the Reformation. They believed that the Puritans, who remained inside the Church of England to and
beyond this date, were in a worse state than they, for the
Puritans had been vouchsafed the light and did not follow
its gleam. Their immediate neighbors to the north of
Scrooby were Catholics. There was but one thing to do—to
leave England and seek salvation in a new land.

Their difficult journey to Holland, their uncomfortable
stay there, the insidious threat presented by the beliefs and
practices of Netherlanders no more in accord with their
tenets than their English neighbors had been, the breath-
taking decision to seek out an isolated Zion in the wilderness, the finding of it, and the epic story of its perilous years
are a tale no less inspiring than familiar, but not a tale over
which we must pause. One aspect of it, an aspect less
stressed than most because on the surface it seems less
dramatic, is important to our purpose. When the Pilgrims
sailed for America, the Puritans were still inside the Church
of England. The Puritans of Massachusetts Bay were the
sons of men who worshiped, with whatever strong misgiv-
ings, within that Church. The Pilgrims not only cut themselves off from England in 1620; they cut themselves off
from the main current of the Protestant Reformation. Thereafter they were as isolated in a religious sense as they
were in a physical sense. The Reformation continued its
progress, leaving the Pilgrims an island of dissent as static
as it was isolated. There were many reasons why the Plymouth colony did not attract new members as did the Mas-

sachusetts Bay colony. One reason was that in the decades after 1620 there was in England no residue that shared the Pilgrim viewpoint from which to draw.

The Pilgrims brought into being at Plymouth their version of the Church-State. It was by design and in achievement the ecclesiastical and political community where they could live the godly life that their consciences and convictions dictated. The physical austerities were implicit in life on the fringe of a wilderness. The moral and social austerities were of their own choosing, and the sternness of their code should not be judged by the standards of a century that does not accept it, but by the spirit of men and women whose burning conviction it was that they must and would embrace it. Spartan austerity ceases to be Spartan in the metaphoric sense when willingly accepted by Spartans. It is Spartan only when imposed on Athenians.

In 1627, the Year of Deliverance, a permanent land-assignment system was worked out. In the same year it was officially recognized that there were people in the colony who were not of it. The aliens of Plymouth were either non-members of the Church or members of other dissenter sects. The Church, however, was not identical with the congregation. The Church consisted of those adults consecrated to God's service and prepared to testify to their faith. The Church governed and disciplined all. The congregation consisted of all the rest except those theological waifs and strays who somehow happened into Plymouth. In point of theology the Pilgrims were thoroughgoing Calvinists, holding to predestination and the doctrine of the elect. They rejected the surplice, but the ministers and elders wore black gowns with white bands. The Pilgrims called their ministers, subjecting their faith, devotion, and godliness to the most acid tests. The test administered to one of the laity who aspired to membership in the Church was scarcely less searching. It is, perhaps, accurate to say that they rather grudgingly tolerated those of other creeds. In the human sense their hospitality was admirable; sometimes they gave months of protection to those wanderers who, in ways that now border on the inexplicable, found their way to Plymouth. They did so in a spirit of human compassion and not as a matter of deliberate policy. As other settlements were founded along the coast, they gradually shut their doors to those not of their own convictions. The day when toleration was deemed a virtue had not yet dawned.

The Pilgrims had come to the New World for freedom to worship God in their own way. As a logical corollary their State was a church. The corollary to this was that the church leaders had full authority over the State, including the very necessary and desirable authority to regulate and limit the growth of the colony. Plymouth wanted none but potential members of the Church, and for the reason already suggested they were hard to come by. As time passed, Plymouth, the first of the Puritan colonies, was the least and weakest in numbers. Until Plymouth was assimilated into the expanding Massachusetts Bay colony, it continued to be what it had been from the beginning, a static and isolated island of dissent past which the current of the Reformation had swept.

THE LEVELS OF CITIZENSHIP

The determination to maintain unchanged the Church-State of their convictions led to various levels of citizenship and non-citizenship in the Plymouth colony. It is no exaggeration to say that at first Governor Bradford was the government—a wise, farsighted, and humane government. As time passed, the government came to include the General Court, a devout, prudent, sober, tightly compact company of church members. Known after 1630 as Freemen, they

were probably as few as fifteen in the early years; they numbered sixty-eight in 1633, when the first list of them was
compiled, and were fewer than two hundred in 1659. This
was the electorate of the Plymouth colony.

Below the Freeman were the Inhabitants. An Inhabitant
was a potential Freeman. He was the head of a family, a
property owner, and a permanent resident. He could not
vote, but he had rights to land and other property and
certain civic duties, which included attendance at church
and military service. Wives and children had the legal
status of their husbands and fathers.

Below the Inhabitants were the Sojourners. They had
no legals right nor civil equality; their residence was tem-
porary and at the governor's discretion. However, they were
Inhabitants and even Freemen *in posse*. By proving themselves to the governor and the general court, they could
aspire to the lower and then the upper level of citizenship.
Below the Sojourners were the indentured white servants,
the domestic servants who were not indentured, the appren-
tices, and the Indians who lived in Plymouth. Taken collectively, they comprised perhaps as much as a quarter of
the population, although they decreased percentagewise as
time passed.

Thus Plymouth was a Church-State ruled by a governor
and a small and highly select theological aristocracy, a
Church-State with various grades of citizenship and non-
citizenship. It was like Calvin's Geneva in a few respects,
very different from it in many others. Our knowledge of it
is dependent very largely on Bradford's *Of Plimoth Plan-
tation*, but Bradford did not write a church history and
many deductions must be inferential. It was certainly not
the democracy which it has often been proclaimed, but it
was another of those fertile seedbeds of democracy which
Calvinism planted. Although it stood aloof from the far
stronger colony immediately to the north, Plymouth was

of great importance to it. The experience of the Pilgrims was the guiding norm in the preparations of the Massachusetts Bay Puritans, and at least six guarantors of the Bay colony were members of the Merchant Adventurers who financed the Pilgrims. Plymouth was passed almost immediately by the Boston colony, and within a very few years it was the least of all the plantations that lined the New England coast and the Connecticut valley. Plymouth lived its years of independence on harmonious terms with its far stronger neighbor to the north. Its assimilation by the Massachusetts Bay colony was less a political act than the final, easy completion of a natural process. By 1691 Plymouth ceased to exist as a colony. Yet there is a viewpoint from which Plymouth was never so important as when it ceased to exist. The Pilgrim concept of the relations of Church and State did not cease to exist when Plymouth ceased to exist. It was the Pilgrim concept of the Church and the Pilgrim concept of the Church-State which became, with due modifications and full allowance for other factors, the New England Puritan concept and thus one of the prime factors in the American concept. Tiny Plymouth was the leaven of one of the two major masses in the politico-religious life of colonial America.

THE PURITAN HERITAGE

Among the many and diversified components which make up Americanism, Puritanism looms impressively. It is the first important component to appear, and it has shown powers of endurance equal to any of the others and powers of pervasiveness that surpass most. It has changed to spirits, attitudes, and beliefs at which seventeenth-century Puritans would recoil in horror, even though a merciful Providence would shield them from recognizing their ideological offspring. In the limited field of theology alone, Puritanism produced the emotionalism of the revival and the camp meeting, and it produced the rationalizing of Unitarianism. But Puritanism was not the evangelical camp meeting, nor was it Unitarianism, and treatises on Puritanism written from either assumption merely becloud the issue. Just as there were seeds in Puritanism from which later Methodism and Unitarianism grew, so there were in Puritanism the seeds of religious liberty, political democracy, the economics of rugged individualism and *laissez faire*. But the Puritans would have called down the fires of Gehenna upon *laissez faire* and rugged individualism, on political democracy and religious liberty, had such abominations in the eyes of the Lord contaminated the Massachusetts scene. As for Methodists and Unitarians, had the seventeenth century known such, a vigorous whipping and a stern injunction to depart forever more would have been their lot, with the likelihood of a hanging on Boston Common if they returned. The Puritans believed in religious liberty for Puritans alone; they believed in the Church-State ruled on theocratic principles, and they believed in full government regulation of economic life. Theologically, they believed the doctrine of John Calvin, with important modifications of their own. Most of their economic and political beliefs did not stem from the fact that they were Puritans. Such beliefs, along with their attitude toward religious toleration, stemmed from the fact that they lived in the seventeenth century and shared to the full its beliefs and attitudes.

It is also important to an understanding of the New England Puritans that when they left England, they did not have the attitude of the Pilgrims toward the Church of England. They regarded it as a "true church," by the Calvinistic definition, although a true church sadly corrupted by Catholic survivals and the insistence of the crown upon an episcopacy. They were as prompt as the Church of

England to reject and to uproot with violence any theology based on the concept of direct, personal revelation from God, whether the concept of the inner light as advanced by Anne Hutchinson and her followers in 1636 or by the Quakers in the 1650s. They held, as did the Church of England, to the medieval concept of the unity of life, with men's actions and institutions ascending in a graduated scale of values until they reached the only final and eternal value, the glory of God. But such a concept of the unity of life necessarily implied a complete integration of society, a regimentation of society if one would use a modern term which to the Puritans would not be a term of reproach. Except for a few visionaries and enthusiasts who were shunted into that convenient isolation ward, Rhode Island, the New England theocracy was as close to being totally accepted as any concept can be in mortal life. It was not until the seventeenth century was close to its end that strange horns began to blow outside the walls of the Puritan Jericho.

GOVERNMENT VERSUS ORIGINAL SIN

The Puritan Church-State was built in Massachusetts for religious reasons, by men and women who believed that the Church and the State were integral and one. In the Puritan theory of the State, government is a logical consequence of original sin. As a result of Adam's fall, sin entered life. Government came into being to curb sin, which threatens not only souls but also lives and property. More accurately, it was brought into being by God for that purpose although God did not decree what form government should take. He did ordain that men should live a community life in submission to authority, and that authority should be vigilant in enforcing His law. The trapper and the frontiersman were not Puritans. Long after the French had penetrated to the Rocky Mountains and the Gulf of Mexico, the Puritan Far West started at the Connecticut River.

In the Puritan Church-State there was no thought of human equality. The Church-State was ruled by the elect, and all who resided within the Church-State were to accept their rule or suffer the consequences. It is rather unrealistic to berate the Puritans for not permitting religious toleration since they had come to Massachusetts to avoid it. In 1681 a tiny group of Anabaptists established a beachhead at Charlestown, Massachusetts. When they appealed to the elect for religious toleration, Samuel Willard, minister of the Third Church in Boston, cleared their misunderstandings about the motives of the Puritans in coming to the New World: "I perceive they are mistaken in the design of our first Planters, whose business was not Toleration; but were professed enemies of it, and could leave the World professing they died *no Libertines*. Their business was to settle, and (as much as in them lay) secure Religion to Posterity, according to that way which they believed was of God."[1]

The Puritan Church-State accepted, however, certain axioms not accepted at Geneva. These axioms, ruled by fundamental law and the social compact, developed naturally out of the English history of Puritanism. In the mother country the Puritans had sided with the Parliament against the sovereigns and the bishops. Consequently they had accepted the Parliamentary thesis that there is a fundamental law under which the ruler must govern and that government comes into being by a compact of the governed. The fundamental law is in the Bible; it is clear and definite and its injunctions are binding on all, including the rulers. Where the Bible is silent, men are free to create their own fundamental law, but men are certainly not free to disregard it once it has been created. The concept that society comes into being by a compact also rested on a theological foundation.

Man in a state of sin is in a state of bondage. The elect to whom God gives His grace are freed from bondage. This freedom carries the unimaginable reward of eternal salvation; it carries also the duty of ruling the Church-State by the fundamental law of God. All must go to church, but membership in the Church is restricted to those able to prove their regeneration. Having been freed from the bondage of sin, they are free to enter the Church and to assume the obligations of the Church-State. Thus the Puritan Church-State rested on a voluntary compact entered upon by those to whom God has vouchsafed His grace. In return for their voluntary assumption of their duties, God grants them salvation. Man brings the Church-State into being, but it is the Church-State ordained by God Who uses His elect as His effective agents in its operation.

The best single expression of the concept in colonial literature is to be found in the speech delivered to the General Court by John Winthrop on July 3, 1645. Winthrop had become embroiled in a dispute in the town of Hingham. He was impeached for exceeding his authority, was tried and acquitted. His address subsequent to his acquittal is a gem of Puritan philosophy. He points out that the point at issue concerned the authority of the magistrates and the liberty of the people. He states that although the people call the magistrates, their power comes from God: "It is yourselves who have called us to this office, and being called by you, we have our authority from God, in way of an ordinance, such as hath the image of God eminently stamped upon it, the contempt and violation whereof hath been vindicated with examples of divine vengeance. . . . The covenant between you and us is the oath you have taken of us, which is to this purpose, that we shall govern you and judge your causes by the rules of God's laws and our own, according to our best skill." It is the duty of the magistrates to govern according to the fundamental law of God. If they err in matters that are plain, they must bear the consequences, but if they err in matters that are not plain, the people must accept the fact in a spirit of submission.

Two Kinds of Liberty

Winthrop further points out that there are two kinds of liberty, the liberty of brutes and "the other kind of liberty I call civil or federal." The liberty of brutes is incompatible with authority, and its exercise only brutalizes men. "This is that great enemy of truth and peace, that wild beast, which all the ordinances of God are bent against, to restrain and subdue it." Civil or federal liberty might also be called moral liberty, "in reference to the covenant between God and man, in the moral law, and the politic covenants and constitutions, amongst men themselves." Such liberty is the proper end of authority and society cannot exist without it; it is the liberty that protects men's lives and goods. "This liberty is maintained and exercised in a way of subjection to authority; it is of the same kind of liberty wherewith Christ hath made us free. The woman's own choice makes such a man her husband; yet being so chosen, he is her lord, and she is subject to him, yet in a way of liberty, not of bondage; and a true wife accounts her subjection her honor and freedom, and would not think her condition safe and free, but in her subjection to her husband's authority. Such is the liberty of the church under the authority of Christ, her king and husband. . . . Even so, brethren, it will be between you and your magistrates. If you stand for your natural corrupt liberties, and will do what is good in your own eyes, you will not endure the least weight of authority, but will murmur, and oppose, and be always striving to shake off that yoke; but if you will be satisfied to enjoy such civil and lawful liberties, such as Christ allows you, then will you quietly and cheerfully submit unto that authority which is set over you, in all the administrations of it, for your good."[2]

As put into practice the Puritan Church-State rested on a social compact confined to the relatively few elect. The officially sanctified elected the officers and passed the laws, and the system of the Church in determining who were the elect enormously facilitated the system. The elect were the Citizens. Beneath them were the Inhabitants, who had the same property rights and the same rights to society's services and protection as the Citizens, but did not have a voice in the government or in the selection of ministers. Obviously this is the same concept as the Plymouth concept of Freemen and Inhabitants; the Puritan State unquestionably was modeled in large measure on the Pilgrim State. It is equally unquestionable that it was molded in large measure by the history of the English Puritan movement and by the logic of Puritan theology. Where the influence of Plymouth ends and the influences of history and theology begin cannot be determined, nor is the point of major consequence. What is of major consequence is that New England Puritanism resulted in a Church-State ruled by a small and highly select aristocracy of the elect, with grades of citizenship and non-citizenship, even as Plymouth. Church and State were one and inseparable, and the Church completely dominated the State. In it society was stratified and rigid, and society was ruled by theocratic authoritarians. The differences between the Calvinistic Church-State in Europe and in America are dwarfed by the resemblances. Boston was the New World Geneva. By 1640 the New World Geneva had 16,000 inhabitants, and the smaller Genevas that sprang up near New Haven, along the Connecticut River, in central Massachusetts, and along the coasts of New Hampshire and Maine added their thousands more. In one short decade Calvinism in America had grown to such proportions that the Indians, the French, and the Dutch were powerless to contain it. The first important component of the American spirit had been brought into being, the first important factor to consider in the American relationship of Church and State. It was a component, as said before, with powers of endurance equal to any of the others and powers of pervasiveness that have surpassed most.

5

The State Church in the South

We may now turn our attention to the southern colonies. Among the outlying and less heeded precincts of the diocese of the bishop of London in the seventeenth and eighteenth centuries were the colonies of Maryland, Virginia, South Carolina, to some extent North Carolina, and New York, Queens, Richmond, and Westchester counties in New York. In the middle and northern colonies, except in the New York area, neither the bishop of London nor his Church had a legal footing, and the vast area from Maryland to Canada was a missionary field where the Society for Propagating the Gospel strove to spread the Anglican gospel with indifferent success. In New England its efforts, as one would expect, met with stout-hearted and highly vocal opposition. Nowhere, not even in Virginia, where the establishment of the Church of England met with the greatest success, was there at any time anything that bore even the faintest resemblance to the State Church as Henry VIII, Elizabeth, and James I conceived it. Everywhere, in the relationship of Church and State, the Church bore itself with the realistic meekness that befits the poor relation.

Such were the facts, and the theory on which the affairs of the Church of England in the colonies were conducted bears little more than a casual resemblance to them. The bishop of London was the diocesan of the plantations. By what grant of authority the honor fell to him is obscure. One thesis is that the authority was granted to him in an order of the Council issued under Laud, an order which has obstinately refused to reveal its whereabouts. Another thesis is that the extension of his jurisdiction to the southern colonies was a usurpation in the first instance. In either case it was a highly theoretical jurisdiction for many years; as late as 1620 only five clergymen are known to have been in the colony of Virginia. The theological needs of those who settled Virginia, a carefree lot, doubtless were substantially greater than the needs of the elect of Massachusetts, but a more striking contrast could hardly be discovered than the ways in which the respective needs were ministered to.

The first instance of an active interest in the spiritual state of Virginia evidenced by a bishop of London came in 1619, when Bishop John King collected £1000 for the education of the Indians. Bishop King died in 1620, and there is no evidence that his successor took Virginia to be part of his province. However, the Virginia assembly of 1624 put the colony on record as part of the domain of the Established Church, enacting "that there be an uniformity in our Church, as near as may be to the Canons in England, both in substance and circumstance; and tht all persons yield obedience to them under pain of censure."[1] Realistic light on the actual situation is shed by the report to the same assembly that a number of clergymen were officiating in the colony without orders.[2]

In July 1628, William Laud became bishop of London.

By 1632 he submitted recommendations to the Privy Council aimed at extending religious conformity among English subjects overseas. On October 1, 1633, the Council passed an order providing "That the Company of Merchant Adventurers should not hereafter receive any minister into their Churches in foreign parts without his Majesty's approbation in person, and that the Liturgy and Discipline now used in the Church of England should be received and established there, and that in all things concerning their Church Government they should be under the jurisdiction of the Lord Bishops of London as their Diocesan."[3] The context of the order makes it clear that it applied specifically to the churches at Delft and Hamburg which the Company of Merchant Adventurers controlled, and there is no evidence that it was loosely interpreted to include Virginia. The fact remains, however, that Laud did attempt to exercise some control over the Church in Virginia. As is well known, the policies of Laud, which were directed toward unity and conformity at home, were a major factor in promoting the stream of Puritan migration to New England during the fourth decade of the century.

The execution of Laud took place in 1645. His sovereign followed him to the block four years later, and during the Commonwealth any vestige of a connection between the Anglican episcopate and Virginia naturally disappeared. The record of the first fifty-three years of the Virginia colony reveals only two facts of permanent importance to church history in America—the establishment of the Church of England in Virginia and the recognition of the bishop of London as diocesan of the colonies. Neither fact, of course, has an importance even momentarily comparable to the importance of the actual establishment of the Puritan Church-State in New England during approximately the same years.

Religion in Maryland

The early religious history of Maryland is entirely different from that of Virginia. Maryland was the first colony to have a lord proprietor with a royal charter and close to the authority of an independent sovereign. The charter granted "as ample rights, jurisdictions, privileges, prerogatives . . . as used and enjoyed within the bishopric or county palatine of Durham." George Calvert, Lord Baltimore held the charter, but George Calvert was a Catholic. By corollary, Virginia proved inhospitable and he obtained rights to a tract north of the Potomac, a tract which included not only the approximate territory of the present state of Maryland but also modern Delaware and parts of Pennsylvania and West Virginia. The eccentric boundary lines of Maryland and the frequently turbulent relations between Marylanders and their neighbors attest to the less than topographic care with which this document was put together.

George Calvert's aims were to make himself a ruler and his realm a haven for persecuted Catholics. He died before he could carry out his aims, but his son Cecilius was a faithful heir. He brought into being something like a feudal realm, but Maryland held to that character for only a few years. The leaven of democracy was working in the colony; the charter provided that laws be made by the proprietor and the freemen, and by the middle of the seventeenth century the latter had a representative system and a bicameral legislature. What is vastly more important to our purpose, they had religious toleration.

The two original havens for the oppressed in America were Rhode Island and Maryland. It is instructive to observe the very different processes of reasoning which brought them into being. Roger Williams was a man of intense religious conviction and perfervid piety. The very intensity of his conviction, the very fervor of his piety acted in a fascinating way to make him tolerate those of other views. Can one have final certainty about the message of the Lord? What man can say in the face of the Lord that he has devoted every last scintilla of his mind and heart to the understanding of His message, and that the understanding is complete? Furthermore, what is conversion worth at the gunpoint? What is the value of adherence to the truth, when in the background are the stocks and whipping post? Can the Word of the Lord be chained to the political works of men and its supernal beauty stay immaculate? Roger Williams would separate Church and State to preserve the Church from the world's defilement. He believed in religious toleration because he could not tolerate the thought that the love of God be forced.

Cecilius Calvert was a man of sincere but ordinary religious convictions. He had the moral courage to be a Catholic when it took a vast amount of moral courage to hold to the old Church. Like his father he had the political sagacity of the born man of the world, and he could steer his course through the theological and political rocks and reefs and emerge unscathed. His secondary reason for founding the Maryland colony was to provide a haven for his oppressed co-religionists. But he could not provide a haven for them, within the limits of practical politics, unless he also welcomed the Protestant subjects of his Protestant monarch. On nothing more profound than the live-and-let-live thesis, the only thesis on which Catholics could then live in the New World, Maryland became the other home of religious toleration. The principle was embodied in the famous Toleration Act of 1649, which extended toleration to all Christian sects except the Unitarians. They and the Jews were denied full political rights in Maryland until 1826.

Nothing could be further from secularism than the spirit of the Toleration Act. One's Christianity had to be Trinitarian. To speak with disrespect of the Virgin Mary, the apostles, or the evangelists called for a fine, or for a public whipping and imprisonment. To refer to another's religion in a "reproachful manner" called for the same. It was a practical measure, designed to keep the peace in a colony originally Catholic but quickly filling up with Puritans who had attempted to settle in Virginia and had been driven out. The history of religious toleration contains an occasional Roger Williams, but most of its figures are Cecilius Calverts. Temperamentally the men were entirely different and the reasoning processes which brought them to religious toleration were entirely different. However, it is of fundamental importance that each started from a sincere and personal religious conviction. Religious toleration in America sometimes has been the result of thinking marked by the highest spiritual quality. Sometimes it has been the result of thinking marked by the soundest political sagacity. Never in this country has it found its origin in religious indifference, although of course the normal effect of religious indifference has been to support it.

The final victory in Maryland did not rest with religious toleration, although toleration did not meet with a really final defeat. The Cromwellian government sent a commission to Maryland to receive the surrender of the colony. Although Calvert watched the storm clouds with an experienced eye and appointed a Protestant governor, one William Stone, the latter was thrust out of office. Stone bided his time for three years and then, in 1655, with a small army attacked the Puritans at Annapolis. The Battle of the Severn, the most remote of all the echoes from the battles of Roundhead and Cavalier, was a total defeat for Stone. The Puritans were left in complete control of the colony. Already they had suspended the Act of Toleration. They replaced it with a law banning "popery, prelacy, and licentiousness of opinion." The first two are to be translated Catholics and Episcopalians. The blanket term covers both the principle of toleration itself and members of such other creeds as did not accept the principles of Calvinism, notably the Baptists and Quakers.

The Puritan reign in Maryland ended when the Puritan reign ended in England. Lord Baltimore sent his son Charles to govern the colony. Charles Calvert was the first of his family to live in Maryland; Cecilius Calvert's forty years of devotion to Maryland had been extended from his London residence, and he literally never saw his colony. Under Charles Calvert the colony was peaceful, and the Calvert policy of toleration made Maryland a proper haven for Quakers and Huguenots, Dutchmen and Germans. The golden age ended abruptly. The unfortunate death of the messenger sent by Maryland to welcome the accession of William and Mary resulted in his message never being delivered. The Maryland charter was revoked, and Maryland became a royal colony, remaining such from 1691 until 1715. The Church of England was established and the church tax set at forty pounds of tobacco per "poll," be it rich or poor. The colony got the sweepings of the Church of England as its clergymen, and the clergymen got the sweepings of the tobacco sheds as their church tax. Toleration was withdrawn from the Catholics, who now numbered less than 10 per cent of the colony's population and were subjected to considerable persecution. The Puritans also paid much of the price for their day of Calvinistic glory. The Calverts, now safely Episcopalian, were restored in 1715 and remained in control of the colony until the Revolution. During these days the governor and assembly were too preoccupied with political quarrels to have much energy for theological regimenting. Numerically the Church of England was quite strong in Maryland, but for obvious historic reasons the establishment was never so solid there as in Virginia.

THE CAROLINAS AND GEORGIA

The story of the establishment in the other southern colonies can be quickly told. The history of North Carolina starts in a way to make Tar Heels walk on clouds. One may pass over the gracious grant of land which made the colony include nearly all of what is now the United States south of Virginia and west to the Pacific; the colony was equipped at the outset with a constitution drawn up expressly for it by the philosopher John Locke. The Fundamental Constitutions or Grand Model was a document less democratic than one would expect from the pen of Locke, but Locke was in the service of Anthony Ashley Cooper, Earl of Shaftesbury, one of the grantees, and Shaftesbury may have been less given to the ideals of democracy than Dryden's outraged strictures in *Absalom and Achitophel* would indicate. Actually the Grand Model provided a landed aristocracy of earls, barons, and proprietors. Two fifths of the land was to be theirs, and the remaining three fifths was graciously granted to tenants on terms amounting to serfdom. The Grand Model limped to a speedy and total collapse, and with it collapsed its one progressive clause. Religious toleration was provided for all except Catholics by it. Thereafter the Church of England was established in North Carolina, but the establishment was very incomplete and very weak. The important physical fact that North Carolina had no important seaport hindered its development and made it rather a secondary development from the other colonies. It was and long remained a land of frontiersmen who made their worship in God's open cathedral, and probably little enough of that.

South Carolina also started with the dubious benefit of the Grand Model and was not separated politically from North Carolina until 1729. What difference there was in the development of the Church in South and North Carolina arose fundamentally from the physical differences between the colonies. South Carolina had its excellent seaport at Charleston. This speedily became one of the important mercantile and cultural centers of the colonies. South Carolina had far fewer mountains, valleys, and forests than North Carolina, and consequently fewer frontiersmen. South Carolina offered far more of the conditions under which the Established Church could prosper than did North Carolina, and it did prosper much better in the old south state. But not even in South Carolina, the colony most like Virginia in spirit, was the Established Church comparable in strength to the Church in Virginia.

The founding of Georgia lies outside the period here considered. When Oglethorpe reached the mouth of the Savannah in 1733, he brought with him a charter granting freedom of religion to all but Catholics. He further brought instructions to build a military barrier that would protect South Carolina from Spanish Florida. Throughout the colonial period Georgia was a frontier land like North Carolina, with standards of piety comparable to North Carolina's. As time passed the Establishment was extended to Georgia, but its hold was very partial, and the religious history of the colony of Georgia belongs to the eighteenth century.

Thus the first century of colonization ended with a Calvinistic Church-State firmly founded in New England. Growing with only the most nominal opposition and that internal, it was as absolute a theocracy as the world has known. The two ultimate monuments to Calvinism are Geneva and Boston. The century ended with the Church

of England established in the southern colonies. It was
strongest in Virginia, but the term is only relative. Actually
the State Church of Virginia was a pale simulacrum of the
State Church of Elizabeth's England, and even that, as has
been seen, did not exist for reasons primarily religious. The
Established Church in the southern colonies had no bishops
nor ecclesiastical courts, and the very nature of the establishment differed from colony to colony. The Church enjoyed the favor of the colonial governors but it lacked the
one pearl without price which the Congregational Church
had. No Anglican ever left England to secure freedom of
worship; no Virginia Episcopalian had the fervent motivation of a Massachusetts Puritan. In Massachusetts the
Church was the State. In Virginia and, to a lesser degree,
in the rest of the South the Church was formally part of
the State although hardly a part that loomed large in southern minds.

To reconcile these utterly opposed religious traditions and
attitudes was to be part of the task of the Founding Fathers
yet unborn. To reconcile with both the religious traditions
and attitudes of the middle colonies, where from the start
there was a religious confusion that is typically American,
was a task only slightly less difficult. It cannot be stressed
too strongly that the American principle of the separation
of Church and State did not arise from secularism nor from
the withering away of religion's drooping vine. It arose
in the United States for the same fundamental reason that
it arose in the colony of Maryland. Only by separating
Church and State and barring any religious establishment
could there be religious peace.

6

New York and Pennsylvania: Church and State

The relations of Church and State in the colony of New York developed in a fashion quite different from the patterns that emerged in New England and in the South. In New York an English pattern was superimposed on a Dutch pattern, with a resulting pattern not entirely different from the one in Maryland. Much of the time a fair degree of religious toleration was maintained in New York, but the reasoning behind it was closer to that of Cecilius Calvert than to that of Roger Williams.

The religious history of New York may be said to start with the Union of Utrecht, in 1581. The newly created Dutch republic included religious toleration as Article 13 of its fundamental laws. Under this policy the new and tiny nation flourished and ceased to be tiny. In three decades Holland had a population almost as large as that of England, and along with its burgeoning industry and trade, religious toleration was a factor in its growth. The Pilgrims were not the only ones to seek religious freedom for themselves within the hospitable borders of the Netherlands.

The Dutch Church, in 1569, had adopted the Presbyterian system, with some modifications of its own. All the members of the Church in a given city were considered to belong to a single congregation. The ministers rotated among the churches, and so did their flock. Each province controlled its own church affairs, and all met in general synod each three years. By 1581 the Reformed Church of Holland was an accomplished fact and had become the State Church. It faced almost at once the challenge of Jacob Arminius, who rejected unconditional election and advocated unlimited atonement. The triumph over Arminianism, climaxed by the Council of Dort in 1618–19, was a triumph for undiluted, if not indeed for concentrated Calvinism. The death of Prince Maurice in 1625, however, brought religious relief to the followers of Arminius, and full toleration was thereafter accorded them.

As a consequence of the habitual policy of toleration accepted by the Dutch, the search for religious freedom was not a factor in the Dutch settlement of New Netherland. Willem Usselinx, founder of the Dutch and Swedish West India Companies, was a thoroughgoing Calvinist, but his company was more interested in beaver skins than human souls. Religion made a rather tardy appearance in the new colony, three years elapsing between the first settlement and the appearance of organized religion. When it did come, it came under the patronage of a member of the French Reformed Church, Peter Minuit, who brought with him the Comforters of the Sick, officials of the Church whose duty it was to aid the ministers of large parishes. By 1628 the pioneer minister was on Manhattan Island and the first church organized in the middle colonies had come into existence, the present Collegiate Reformed Dutch Church of the City of New York. The congregation was partly Dutch and partly French, and services in French

were occasionally conducted. With the settlement of Rens-
selaerwyck in the Albany area the Dutch Church came into
being at the head of navigation.

PETER STUYVESANT

When that vigorous and domineering son of a Dutch
Reformed minister, Peter Stuyvesant, came to the colony
in 1647 as its director general, he found organized religion
in a sadly disorganized state. Within three years he had
straightened things out. The 1640 charter of Freedoms
and Exemptions provided that "No other religion shall be
publicly admitted in New Netherland except the Reformed
. . . and for this purpose the Company shall provide and
maintain good and suitable preachers, schoolmasters, and
Comforters of the Sick."[1] The full record of Stuyvesant's
stalwart services for the Lord is to be found in Frederick J.
Zwierlein's *Religion in New Netherland*.[2] It was marked by
a vigorous persecution of the Quakers, the Lutherans, and
the Jews. Catholics were not a New York factor, and Puritans were tolerated, since their beliefs were in fundamental
agreement with those of the Dutch Church. The company
managed to put a partially effective quietus on Stuyvesant's
enthusiasm, but the Dutch record for religious toleration
was sadly marred during his days of authority.

In 1638 Peter Minuit assisted in the founding of the
Swedish colony on the Delaware River. The following year
the first Lutheran minister reached New World shores,
and not long after, the first Lutheran church was erected
on Tinnicum Island, below present-day Philadelphia. The
happy friendship between the Dutch and Swedes was not
of long duration, and a timely Indian uprising in 1656 did
more than any consideration of Christian comradeship to
divert Stuyvesant's attention from the uprooting of the

Swedes. For some decades Lutheranism held with difficulty its tiny toehold on the shores of the Delaware. In 1696 the Swedish king Charles XI began to take an active interest in the spiritual state of Sweden overseas and sent out three ministers to attend to the community. For the next seventy-five years a great deal of money and devoted effort was expended by the people of Sweden on the American mission, and the caliber of the Lutheran ministers sent out and the quality of their work comprise one of the brightest if very minor aspects of the early religious life of the colonies. The Lutheran Church, however, was not destined to survive in a land where the numerical strength of Lutheranism was still microscopic. Long before the Revolution the Swedish language ceased to be used in church services and gradually the Lutheran churches were absorbed by the Anglican.

Meanwhile New Netherland had become New York. In 1665 New Netherland was ceded to England by the Treaty of Breda. The religious situation was one of the complications facing the new lords of the land. The Dutch Reformed Church was not a dissenter church, but neither was it the Church of England. Sir Edmund Andros showed an intelligent and sympathetic interest in the religious needs of the Dutch, and in 1683 with New York flourishing under Governor Thomas Dongan, the first Irish Catholic governor in New York history, a Charter of Liberties and Privileges was passed. A preponderantly Dutch assembly enacted full religious freedom for all religions in New York, and provided that "all other Christian churches that shall hereafter come and settle within this province shall have the same privilege."[3] In 1693 an effort to establish the Church of England in New York met with scant success. With the overthrow of James II in 1688, the broad toleration envisaged by the enactment of 1683, which included even Catholics, was no longer acceptable to the British throne. After several efforts had been repulsed, in 1693 a measure was pushed through a reluctant and mainly Dutch assembly, which was interpreted, although not without vigorous protest, as establishing the Church of England in New York, Queens, Richmond, and Westchester counties. The only tangible evidence of its operation afforded in the seventeenth century was the granting of a charter in 1697 to Trinity Church. The truth is that Episcopalianism was almost nonexistent in New York at that time, the chaplain of the English garrison reporting in 1695 that his faithful numbered 90 families. He further reported that about half of the 3525 families in the province were Dutch, somewhat less than half were English dissenters, and that the only other group of any numerical impressiveness were the French.[4]

In short, the record of New York confirms the record of Maryland. Except for the days of the exuberant Stuyvesant, New York had a sustained record of religious toleration during the seventeenth century. It arose in the first instance from the admirable background of religious toleration at home which was part of New York's Dutch heritage. It was perpetuated, however, by the fact that New York came speedily to have an important admixture of worshipers at churches other than the Dutch Reformed. When the English took over, they had their choice between religious toleration and the desperate task of converting the stubborn Dutch at the gunpoint. They followed what was then the course of expediency, although the twentieth century honors it in higher terms. When religious toleration first arose in America, it was (always excepting Roger Williams' Rhode Island) one of the virtues which are born of necessity. Where it was not a necessity, as in New England and Virginia, it did not exist. Where it was a necessity, as in Maryland and New York, it existed. Society had not yet reached the point where it was ready to consider toleration as a virtue in itself, but the groundwork was being laid. Religious toleration, like some of humanity's other noble structures, does not rest on a pedestal of flawless marble.

THE STORY OF PENNSYLVANIA

The only colony to rival Massachusetts in distinctiveness of religious tradition is Pennsylvania. It was not without good reason that Calvinism everywhere regarded as a mortal enemy what may, in the broadest of theological terms, be called the Quaker creed. The mortal enemy is not necessarily the man whose thinking is based on axioms entirely different from one's own. He is at least as likely to be the man whose thinking develops from the same axioms, but in a different way. From the axiom that the direct inspiration of God is unmistakable there developed, on the one hand, Calvinism, the Calvinistic Church-State, and the theocracy of Geneva and Boston. From the same axiom there developed the literal and complete separation of Church and State which was at least an ideal among the continental Anabaptists. That same ideal, naturally modified by the English tradition and the possession of a land to develop and organize without interference from a Prince, found expression in Pennsylvania. Implicit in the viewpoint of Luther, which makes no provision for authoritative interpretation, is the principle that the message of Scriptures cannot be misunderstood. At that implicit principle is the great fork in the road; to the right lies Calvinism and the theocratic state, to the left lies democracy and religious tolerance. Philadelphia is on the road to the left.

There is much misunderstanding about the history and beliefs of the Quakers. The very fact that the members of the Society of Friends are universally known as Quakers, a term of opprobrium given to them by their enemies, shows how much of the common belief about the Quakers stems from the statements of such enemies. Originally George Fox did not aim at the creation of a new church. Like the continental reformers and the Puritans, he sought a purified church restored to apostolic simplicity and freedom. A man of great strength of will and humility of heart, George Fox was one of the remote yet important makers of America. At the heart of his doctrine is the belief that every soul is directly responsible to God, without mediation of cleric or church, because the Holy Spirit is present in every heart. "The Lord God opened to me," he says, "by his invisible power how every man was enlightened by the divine light of Christ: I saw it shine through all, and that they who believed in it came out of condemnation into the light of life, and became children of the light; but that they that hated it and did not believe it were condemned by it, though they made a profession of Christ."

The fundamental difference between the Puritan and the Quaker viewpoint lies in the manner in which the Lord extends His divine light. The Puritans believed that He extends it in the form of efficacious grace to His elect. Those who receive it are freed from the bondage of sin and, as free men, enter into the covenant of the Lord. It is their duty to constitute the Church and make effective its society. They are the rulers of the Church-State. The Quakers believed that God extends His divine light to all men, but that it is not efficacious in all men. It is efficacious only in those who receive it, and efficacious reception depends on the heart and not the intellect. Because all men share the Light, the Quakers were instinctive believers in toleration, and so with them toleration was a dictate of principle and not of expediency. Because all men share the Light, the Quakers were instinctive believers in democracy, and the *thou* and *thee* which the seventeenth century reserved for servants and other social inferiors were their general and

democratic terms of address. From the same belief stem
their distinctive forms of worship, their ecclesiastical democracy in which women had equal rights with men, and
other aspects of the Quaker creed and Quaker life which
are not our concern. What is vital to our purpose is that
the Quakers were instinctive believers in democracy and
religious toleration, and that they created Pennsylvania
and much of New Jersey.

Not all the Quakers were of the stamp of George Fox
and William Penn. In many of them the mark of religious
hysteria and the martyr complex are plainly evident, and
one's sympathy often goes, at least in fractional measure,
to the Puritans whose realms they invaded from their
strategic base, the isolation ward of the colonies, Rhode
Island. There seems to have been a genuine fear among the
Puritans that the Quakers had taken their basic ideas from
the violent Anabaptists of Münster, and that violence was
to be feared from the Quakers if they grew strong enough.
The most vigorous measures, including hangings, were taken
to ward off the imaginary peril from New England, and
only the direct intervention of Charles II put an end to
Quaker persecution in New England. In New Amsterdam,
Governor Stuyvesant was checked in his persecution of the
Quakers by the realistically minded Dutch West India
Company, which took no pains to conceal that its belief
in religious toleration was based on expedience: ". . . we
doubt very much if vigorous proceedings against them
ought not to be discontinued, except you intend to check
and destroy your population; which, however, in the youth
of your existence ought rather to be encouraged by all possible means: Wherefore, it is our opinion, that some con-
nivance would be useful; that the conscience of men, at
least, ought ever to remain free and unshackled. Let every-
one be unmolested, as long as he is modest; as long as his
conduct in a political sense is irreproachable; as long as he

does not disturb others, or oppose the government. This maxim of moderation has always been the guide of the magistrates of this city, and the consequence has been that, from every land, people have flocked to this asylum."[5] In the southern colonies there was legislation against the Quakers and some action, but nothing approaching the severity of the action taken in New England. In general, the Quakers made their converts among those in rebellion against the established churches or those who belonged to no church at all. So widespread were their missionary efforts throughout the colonies that the Quakers exercised an influence out of proportion to their actual numbers. The Quakers would be important even if there had been no Pennsylvania.

Quaker Territories

The first Quaker territory in America was in New Jersey. The colony had been divided into West Jersey and East Jersey, the line extending from a point near Delaware Water Gap to a point north of the present Atlantic City, with Princeton close to its mid-point. In 1675 West Jersey passed into Quaker control, and in 1680 East Jersey came partially under Quaker influence. In 1692, however, West Jersey came into the possession of members of the Church of England, and by 1702 Quaker influence had ended in East Jersey. The Quaker rule in New Jersey was of short duration, yet it was not without importance. It gave William Penn and his followers a chance to experiment with government and it brought many Quakers to America. Had it not been for the promise of the New Jersey experiment, it is doubtful if Penn would ever have asked Charles II for the Pennsylvania grant. What that promise meant to America as a whole is well summed up by Professor Sweet: "The

Concessions and agreements of the Proprietors, Freeholders, and Inhabitants of West Jersey, in America, of March, 1677, undoubtedly in large part the work of William Penn, gave to the spirit of liberty a wider range than had heretofore been the case in any record of Anglo-Saxon organic law. It provided for complete liberty of conscience, security from illegal arrest, trial by jury, control of taxation by representatives, elected by a secret ballot of the entire body of proprietors, freeholders, and inhabitants of the colony."

William Penn's wealth and social position made him a potent figure in England in spite of his religious convictions. His friendship with the Duke of York secured him, in March 1681, the grant of the colony of Pennsylvania in payment of the debt of £16,000 which the government owed his father. He threw himself into the task of organizing the colony with all the vigor and ability of a rugged body and an excellent mind, with results that are known to every American. Complete religious toleration was the law in the land of the Quakers, and as a result it speedily became the primary New World haven for the oppressed of many creeds and lands. Quakers, of course, for a long time were in the numerical ascendency. In the earliest days of the colony many Welshmen, mostly Quakers but with an admixture of Baptists and Anglicans, settled west of Philadelphia, leaving their mark in the pleasant suburbs of St. Davids, Berwyn, Bryn Mawr, and Radnor. The Anglicans settled mainly in Philadelphia and for many years filled the executive offices of the government, waging political war against the Quaker legislature. The Anglican illusion that Pennsylvania somehow could be made a northern Virginia, with the Established Church and a bishop who would have the Three Lower Counties, otherwise Delaware, as his manor, died hard. Countless and bewildering German sects found hospitable refuge on Penn's broad acres: Schwenkfelders, Tinkers, Mountain Men and River Brethren, the Labadists, the New Born, and the Society of the Woman in the Wilderness. Germanic mysticism was never quite so rife as in early Pennsylvania, and solitaries with Teutonic names sought out the woods and caves with which Pennsylvania is so liberally blessed. Far and away the most important were the Mennonites, as the more conservative and Quakerlike of the Anabaptists came to be known. The Germans for the most part settled the area extending from Easton through the Lehigh Valley and Lancaster County down to the Maryland line, the Pennsylvania Dutch country of today. Following the sects came great numbers of Lutherans, many of them peasants who sold themselves to the shipping companies to pay their passage. They in turn sold the services of the immigrants and the "redemptioners" paid off their indebtedness by five to ten years of work. All parties deemed it a business transaction without stigma. The Ulstermen began to come after 1700, found the Quakers and their ways distinctly not to their hot-tempered liking, and sought the wilderness where neither papist nor Episcopalian sullied the Presbyterian paradise. As Maryland ceased to be a haven for Catholics, a new haven developed in Pennsylvania, where Catholic churches could be built and the Catholic faith followed without interference. Catholicism was not entirely unopposed in Pennsylvania: Catholics were disfranchised, could not hold public office, and could not conduct schools. Despite these blots on the otherwise noble record of Pennsylvania for toleration in a century when the concept was dangerously new and radical in most minds, Catholics made far better progress in Pennsylvania than in any other colony.

Thus Pennsylvania entered the eighteenth century far in advance of all the other colonies except Rhode Island where concepts of Church and State were concerned. Religious toleration and the absence of an established church were matters of principle in Pennsylvania, and under these principles Pennsylvania flourished. With full allowance for the economic wealth of Philadelphia's hinterland, the leading position of the city in the eighteenth century was due to the intellectual climate that William Penn brought into being and the Quakers faithfully preserved. Benjamin Franklin, America's first son of the Enlightenment, gravitated to Philadelphia as his natural home of the spirit. The American Philosophical Society came into being there in 1743, America's first scientific society and the only one founded in the colonial period. The first American hospital was established there in 1751 and the first systematic teaching of medicine inaugurated. The doors of Pennsylvania were open to the world of men and of ideas, and the eighteenth century entered America through the port of Philadelphia.

In colonial America the opposite poles were Massachusetts and Virginia. Massachusetts presented the Calvinistic Church-State in full development, and Bay State Puritanism was the first important component of Americanism to appear. Virginia did not present the Established Church in anything like a comparable stage of development, but it did present a society with a concept of Church and State antithetical to that of Massachusetts. Could the two have been reconciled into a single nation, granting the full influence of eighteenth-century thinking, had the *tertium quid* been lacking? It took a civil war to do it in England. But the *tertium quid* was not lacking, and America came into being without religious strife. It may well be questioned if any contribution of the middle colonies to the infant nation was quite so important as the tradition of religious toleration and the separation of Church and State. But even as the question is asked, it should be reiterated that religious toleration in New York and Pennsylvania arose out of religious conviction and not religious indifference. In New York it was a policy of the Dutch Reformed Church, a policy in which expediency was an important but not necessarily an unworthy component. In Pennsylvania it was a policy of the Society of Friends that had its very roots in their religious beliefs. It was not accidental that religious toleration flourished best when rooted in the rich soil of the Quaker creed.

7

The Battle of the Bishops

The colonial regions of obvious conflict in matters of Church and State, a conflict that certainly was philosophical and might have become considerably hotter, were Massachusetts and Virginia. There were some theological invasions of the respective regions by Anglican and Puritan groups. Puritans in substantial numbers established beachheads in colonial Virginia and were dislodged, to find refuge in the Calverts' Maryland. Hardly were they settled there, as has been seen, but they set about erecting a Church-State in what had been a land of toleration. Their real future outside New England, however, was reserved for a later date in what would be the states to the west.

The first preparations for an Anglican invasion of New England were made shortly after the Restoration. In 1664 a Royal Commission had sought, with scant success, a modification of the Massachusetts Bay colony's rigid restrictions. After several failures to obtain toleration for Anglicans in the Congregational stronghold, Charles II launched quo warranto proceedings and had the colony charter annulled.

On October 3, 1684, the Massachusetts Bay charter was forfeited and on May 15, 1686, the Reverend Robert Ratcliffe brought Anglicanism into New England. The same year Joseph Dudley brought a royal government to Boston. His successor, Edmund Andros, sought repeatedly the use of a meeting house for Anglican worship. His search was rewarded on Good Friday 1687, when an Anglican service was held in the South Meeting House. The construction of King's Chapel started the next year, but word of the Bloodless Revolution of 1688 brought new hope to beleaguered Congregationalists. Increase Mather was despatched to England to negotiate the return of the old charter. The best he could bring back was a compromise, which included the very distasteful proviso that no religious test could be applied where the right of suffrage was concerned. Through the eighteenth century Anglicanism did not exactly wax in Boston, but neither did it wane. By 1729 there were three Anglican churches in the Hub of the Universe and the heart of Congregationalism. The conquest of Connecticut was both easier and fractionally larger, and in the decade after 1722 over 10 per cent of the graduates of Yale entered the Anglican priesthood.

The Puritans had failed in their efforts to keep the Anglicans out of Zion. They did not fail, until failure had ceased to have a meaning, in their efforts to keep an Anglican bishop out of America. They did not succeed, of course, without substantial assistance from other churches and segments of the population, and probably nothing helped them quite so much as the indifference of the Anglicans of the South. Remote and apparently academic as such a debate may seem, the long-drawn-out battle over the episcopacy was one of the primary factors that led to Article I of the Bill of Rights.

From the Anglican viewpoint the argument in favor of a bishop in the American colonies was unanswerable. In the

Church of England there are certain acts, notably confirmation and ordination, that only a bishop can perform. Without a bishop in the colonies, confirmation as a customary church rite was out of the question. Ordination for a colonist meant going to England, with all the obvious difficulties which that entailed. The logical and far from desirable result was a church whose clergy were partly imported from the mother country and partly recruited, without ordination, from the colonies. The former were not the most pious, diligent, and learned that the Church of England could produce. Neither were the latter. The absence of a bishop meant the absence of proper supervision and disciplinary authority, and the Church of England, with its establishment in the South, where the tradition of piety and churchgoing was most tenuous, suffered severely.

Had the opposition to the presence of an Anglican bishop in the colonies been grounded on nothing more than the desire to hamstring a theological adversary, it would be understandable though nothing more. But it was grounded on something less substantial but far more intricate than that. It will be recalled that to the Puritans of England the Anglican bishops had been vestigial but very active remains of Catholicism, and the active agents of Elizabeth in persecuting Puritans. To the Puritans in America a full Anglican establishment, with bishops, would mean the threat of the same thing. In the middle colonies opposition was centered among the Presbyterians, as would be expected, but it was by no means limited to them. The most potent opposition, however, was to be found in Virginia itself. Here the advocates of the episcopacy had to face the dead weight of inertia, but not altogether a dead inertia. Inertia on occasion can be as determined as its opposite, and this was one of the occasions. Southern inertia did not arise entirely from a lack of religious feeling among southern Anglicans. It must be remembered that many of them were living on or close to the frontier. Frontiersmen do not number among their faults an excessive reverence for panoply and courtly display, and it may be questioned if many of them shared an enthusiasm for giving the Three Lower Counties, alias Delaware, to an Anglican bishop for his episcopal dignity and comfort and that of his retinue. Probably the typical southern attitude, at its best, was expressed by the Virginia planter Robert Carter in a letter written to his London agent in 1720: "Let others take what courses they please in the bringing up of their posterity. I resolve the principles of our holy religion shall be instilled into mine betimes; as I am of the Church of England way, so I desire they shall be. But the high-flown up notions, and the great stress that is laid upon ceremonies, any farther than decency and conformity, are what I cannot come into the reason of. Practical godliness is the substance—these are but the shell."[1]

PRESBYTERIAN AND CONGREGATIONALIST OPPOSITION

The result was that no success attended the efforts of the Anglicans to establish a colonial bishopric. The efforts were made almost exclusively by Anglicans in colonies where Anglicanism was weakest, the New England and Middle Atlantic colonies. Where support might be effective, in Virginia and the colonies to the south, support was not forthcoming. By late in the century the issue had reached the newspaper stage, with the journalistic pyrotechnics which a religious issue with political overtones can summon forth in a century more blasé than the eighteenth. In the ten years before the Revolution the threat of a bishopric had brought together the New England Congregationalists and the middle-colony Presbyterians in a series of conventions and a joint stand, which was presented to the British Government. No opposition was expressed to "harmless and inoffensive bishops," which must be translated as bishops who attend to churchly duties and nothing more. The opposition was clearly expressed to the introduction to America of bishops with political as well as ecclesiastical authority, and to the gradual extension of the Anglican establishment to all the colonies.

Today the fears of the dissenters seem ridiculous. An important corrective, however, must be borne in mind. There was an ideological time lag between the colonies and the mother country. The clock had not moved so quickly in the churches of New England as it had in the council chambers of Old England, nor was the Puritan Church-State entirely a thing of history. Seventeenth-century thinking persisted long and strong in the old Puritan stronghold. Furthermore, seventeenth-century thinking was steadily reinforced by the immigration into the middle colonies of Ulster Presbyterians who still bore clearly visible the marks of John Knox and his Kirk. It may have been an idle fear, but it was an honest one. The proof is that when the Revolution was won, the Anglican Church established its bishoprics without a vestige of opposition from the dissenter churches. Once America was independent and the veto on an established church was written into the Constitution, the specter of a State Church was laid and with it the fear of the Anglican episcopacy.

One of the factors in the immensely intricate equation which was solved by the American Revolution was the quarrel over bishops. It had the effect, perhaps an effect more tended toward than realized, of drawing all Americans into two great, opposing religious camps. It renewed in the dissenter camp fears that had been dormant for decades, but were still alive. John Adams, writing on the causes of the Revolution, had this to say about the controversy: "If any gentleman supposes this controversy to be nothing to the present purpose, he is grossly mistaken. It

spread an universal alarm against the authority of Parliament. It excited a general and just apprehension, that
bishops, and dioceses, and churches, and priests, and
tithes, were to be imposed on us by Parliament. It was
known that neither king, nor ministry, nor archbishops,
could appoint bishops in America, without an act of Parliament; and if Parliament could tax us, they could establish
the Church of England, with all its creeds, articles, tests,
ceremonies, and tithes, and prohibit all other churches, as
conventicles and schism shops."[2]

It would be stretching things too far to say that the
needs of the Church as well as the needs of the State evoked
the Declaration of Independence. The most that the available evidence indicates is that the religious issue between the
majority of the colonists and the Established Church buttressed the political and economic causes of the Revolution.
But buttress them it did, nor is it accidental that the
alignment of the dissenter churches against the Church of
England on this politico-ecclesiastical issue, an alignment
that was emotionally fortified by the sound and fury of a
pre-Revolutionary journalistic debate, found expression in
the first article of the Bill of Rights. To the men of the
eighteenth century the prohibition of an established church
meant freedom for religion, not freedom from religion. It
was rooted, as religious toleration always has been in
America, in the rich soil of religion and not in the thin air
of indifference.

8

The Great Awakening

The major cleavage between the churches in colonial America separated Anglican from dissenter and was present from the start. The effect of it depended on local conditions. Where the minority was too small to make its viewpoint effective, as in Massachusetts and Virginia, there was an established church. Where the minority viewpoint was sufficiently strong to bear effective weight, as in New York, there was religious toleration. The minority viewpoint, whether held by Anglican, Congregationalist, Presbyterian, or Catholic, always was for toleration. There was toleration as a matter of principle only in Rhode Island and Pennsylvania.

The major cleavage by itself would have been enough to insure, within the realities of politics, the absence of an established church and the presence of religious toleration in the United States of the Founding Fathers. But the major cleavage was substantially reinforced by all the minor cleavages which resulted in the pre-Revolutionary period from the Great Awakening. After the Great Awakening, as the lines of the Methodists began to form, not even the ranks of the Congregationalists and the Anglicans were firm and serried, and basic rifts appeared among the Presbyterians and the Baptists. Those who spoke with the tongues were so many and so diverse that the common denominator of disestablishment and toleration became a metaphysical certainty.

It is natural to stress the natures and beliefs of those who were within the several folds during the colonial period. It is dangerously simple to overlook the many who were outside them all. Membership in the various churches was an individual matter in the colonies and never the matter of course it usually was in Europe. Membership in the Congregational churches of New England was a privilege not lightly to be won, and many were left in outer darkness. The same was true in the churches which practiced adult baptism. The same, on other grounds which included the practical impossibility of receiving confirmation, was true in the Anglican South. Add to all this the frontier.

There is no component in the equation quite so important as the frontier. We speak of the settled parts of the colonies and tend to overlook how different was the meaning of the term in the seventeenth and eighteenth centuries from its meaning today. Settlements were small and isolated, even in the "settled parts," except along the immediate seaboard. Means of communication were sparse, conditions of travel were austere. The frontiersman neither expected the organized services of society nor had them. In very large measure he was his own government in a land where rugged individualism was a prerequisite for survival. Granted the conditions of frontier living and the psychology of the frontier dweller, and religion inevitably became in the main an individual matter. There were those who kept in their isolated cabins the pious practices of family worship, but there were many more who forgot them. Taken all in all, it would have been one of the major miracles if the majority of colonial Americans had been churchgoers.

The result was a missionary field of dry tinder for those who could kindle the religious spark. The hearts most receptive to the spark were to be found in the middle colonies, with their background of inner and personal religion. The first major figure in the revivalist movement appeared there. He was Theodore J. Frelinghuysen of the Raritan Valley in New Jersey. Working with emotional and fiery eloquence among the poorer and the younger of the Dutch, he split the Dutch Reformed Church down the middle. On one side of the rift were the older, the more staid, the better off. On the other side were the younger, the more enthusiastic, the less wealthy. Eventually his revival movement won for his party the majority, yet almost to the days of the Revolution the Dutch Reformed Church was in a state of serious schism.

GEORGE WHITEFIELD

The next to catch the spark were the Scotch-Irish of Pennsylvania. It is a far cry yet a clear one from William Tennent's Log College at Neshaminy, Pennsylvania, to the cloistered Gothic of today's Princeton University. In the two decades between 1726 and 1746 Tennent trained a bare handful of men for the Presbyterian ministry, but in each of them the flame of evangelical zeal soared high and hot. These Log College men were the spiritual begetters of still more believers; they spread into New Jersey, took over pulpits wherever there were Scotch-Irish Presbyterians, and soon met the inevitable counterforce. Older men of Scottish training tried to curb the revivalistic neophytes by a diploma requirement; to occupy a Presbyterian pulpit, one had to have a diploma from a European or a New England

college. Either guaranteed a theology marked by more of
the pale cast of thought than was evident in the harangues
of Log College revivalists. The issue was in the balance
when George Whitefield appeared.

That Whitefield was the greatest revivalist of his time
no one questions. That he was the greatest revivalist of all
time some maintain. He was a man apart from the other
evangelists. For one thing, he had a catholicity of spirit that
let him co-operate with any church intent on the salvation of
human souls. He found his most enthusiastic support among
the Log College Presbyterians, but the fires of his eloquence,
which first enkindled the New Jersey plains, were destined
to blaze in all the colonies. Nothing stopped them except the
wall of Catholicism which the French had built in Canada
and the Spaniards in Florida. Emotionalism and eloquence
were the essence of Whitefield, but there must have been
something more. If ever there was a man not to be swayed
by emotionalism nor transported by eloquence, it was Benjamin Franklin. Yet Franklin was Whitefield's loyal and admir-
ing friend for life, and the publisher of his sermons and
journals.

The final result of Whitefield's work, in the terms of
concern to us, was exactly such a rift in Presbyterian ranks
as Frelinghuysen produced among the Dutch. The formal
cleavage came in 1741 at the Philadelphia Synod, where an
anti-revivalistic majority expelled the New Brunswick Pres-
bytery. The revivalists formed the Synod of New York, and
for years the New Side Synod and the Old Side Synod
battled each other with a vigor as strong as they employed
against Satan and his cohorts. The chief existing monument
to the New Side Synod of New York is the College of New
Jersey, otherwise Princeton University, founded in 1746.
Princeton's first five presidents were revivalist preachers,
two of them Log College men. Slowly the New Side won
the field, and before the Revolution the Old Side warded

off extinction only by merger. Cleavage had done its work. There could be no establishment in terms of a Presbyterianism in which the wounds were so deep and fresh, and the healing so recent and so little advanced.

The great importance of the Great Awakening as it affected New England is to be found in the fact that it was the first serious and even successful religious challenge to New England Calvinism. Coupled with the changes in the Massachusetts charter imposed by the Crown, it brought to an end the Calvinistic Church-State in the full sense, although in a modified sense the reign of the Church-State would not end until well after the Revolution.

Jonathan Edwards

The chief figure of the Great Awakening in New England was Jonathan Edwards of Northampton. Edwards was a revivalist with a difference, and the difference was in the direction of the theological rationalizing of the New Englanders and away from the emotional fervors of the Log College graduates. Revivalism was never a product of Calvinism, except by way of reaction. It was the direct product of the personal, pietistic religious tradition of Quakerism and, in general, of the German sects of the middle colonies. But many of the revival manifestations were evidenced during Jonathan Edwards' heyday in Northampton, including conversions by wholesale, the symptoms of mass hysteria on a few occasions, and suicide by despondent sinners on more than one. In this, Jonathan Edwards but fertilized the field for the seed George Whitefield was to sow. When Whitefield preached in New England, the novelty of his extemporaneous manner and the extraordinary difference between his emotional eloquence and the hard and arid dialectic theology to which New Englanders were accustomed from Calvinistic pulpits brought throngs to hear him from the farthest reaches of Yankeedom. Crowds of three and four thousand are recorded, gathered to get their "first taste of the theatre under the flag of salvation," in the words of Ola E. Winslow.[1]

Jonathan Edwards was probably the finest single product of New England Calvinism. George Whitefield was certainly the finest revivalist in colonial history. Their eloquence and fervor set a precedent packed with dynamite. The sort of theology ordinarily heard from Calvinistic pulpits was within the reach only of the professionally trained. It was a disciplined preaching, as befitted a disciplined church. But the emotional eloquence of an Edwards or a Whitefield could be imitated, in its superficial and dramatic aspects, by any ranter and roarer. Within a year the imitators ranted and roared, as the followers gathered and gaped. Of one, the cultivated Dr. Cutler of Christ Episcopal Church in Boston mused, "In the dreadfullest winter I ever saw, people wallowed in the snow night and day, for the benefit of his beastly brayings." But these "beastly brayings" carried the day among the Dutch and the Presbyterians in the middle colonies, and the old-line Calvinists could recognize a hurricane signal. A general convention was called in 1743 by the Congregational ministers, and the errors of revivalism were formally listed. A Testimony denouncing them was published and was shortly subscribed to by 113 ministers from all parts of New England. In Connecticut, legal action was taken against the revivalists, their churches were deprived of legal status, and some of the preachers were thrown into jail.

The great importance of the Great Awakening in New England arose, as has been said, from its successful challenge to Calvinism, a challenge which was the stronger for following the changes in the Massachusetts charter. The spirit of the Church-State to some degree survived, but the fact of the Church-State was passing into history. The Great

Awakening brought into the New England churches a host of converts that may have numbered as many as 50,000. It brought into being between 1740 and 1760 one hundred and fifty new Congregational churches and added to the number of Separatist and Baptist churches. It brought the personal and pietistic religious tradition into a section previously dominated without challenge by Calvinistic rationalization. The further history of that cleavage belongs to the history of religion and not to the history of the Church and State relationship. Suffice it to say that the cleavage in New England, like the cleavage in the middle colonies, made more nearly inevitable the separation of Church and State and the disestablishment of all the churches in the days ahead when a new nation would come into being. As always and everywhere, the New England situation shows that such separation and disestablishment arose out of religion and not its opposite.

AWAKENING IN THE SOUTH

In the South the Great Awakening bore certain specialized characteristics. It was interdenominational, bore the mark of the frontier, and gave to the Baptist and Methodist churches the first increase in that dramatic and continuing process of growth which before long made them outnumber all the other Christian churches in America. But before it came to the Baptists and Methodists, the Great Awakening overtook the Presbyterians.

The revival movement among the southern Presbyterians was an extension of the movement that started in the Raritan Valley of New Jersey and extended wherever there were Presbyterians in the middle colonies. The Presbyterians of the southern colonies lived along or close to that long spinal column of eastern America, the Appalachians. They had moved down the long and fertile valleys stretching south-west of Pennsylvania; the movement was a racial penetration partly Scotch-Irish and partly German. Thus there came into being a western Virginia that was different in racial composition, religion, and economic status from the Virginia long since established by Episcopalians of English descent who had settled the Tidewater and colonized the Piedmont. The Scotch-Irish were true sons of John Knox and the Kirk, and the Germans were pietists and readily receptive to evangelism. In the winter of 1742–43 the Log College sent ministers of the Word to farthermost Virginia. The seed fell on fertile though hilly ground, and wave after wave of revivalism swept down the Shenandoah Valley and the valleys parallel and beyond. The central figure in revival-istic Presbyterianism in the South was a Log College graduate named Samuel Davies. Shrewdly avoiding an attack upon the Established Church, few members of which were to be found so far west as Scotch-Irish Virginia, he devoted himself to his true business with eloquence, intelli-gence, and devotion. As usual in fields so competitive as religion, his very success bred its own perils. Without seek-ing the role, Davies found himself leading the fight for religious toleration in Virginia. The role was forced upon him by the bitter opposition of the Anglican clergy.

It has been seen that again and again in American colonial history religious toleration has been the compromise effected as a result of religious competition. In Virginia there had been no such rivalry until the Presbyterians and the pietists pouring down the western valleys provided the tinder and the revival movement, the spark. Once the blaze of revival-ism was fierce enough to perturb the Established Church, the fight was on. The first battle was fought over the ques-tion of the application of the Act of Toleration of 1689 to Virginia. Davies acted as attorney for the Presbyterians in arguing the case before the general court. The government, otherwise the Anglican, case was presented by Attorney General Peyton Randolph. Davies convinced the majority of the court, against the opposition of Randolph, that the Act of Toleration did apply to Virginia. The second conflict was a long one of attrition; the practical question of how many meeting houses a Presbyterian minister might serve had to be answered in practical terms if Presbyterianism was to flourish in western Virginia. At long last the sons of Knox won the day. By 1755 there were six New Light congregations in Virginia, and Presbyterianism was steadily growing. Four years later Davies was called to Princeton to succeed Jonathan Edwards as president of the College of New Jersey. His work in Virginia had been well done. Presbyterianism there, in the Carolinas, in the lands to the south and west continued to grow in its normal and unimpeded way. The story of that growth is not our concern. What is very much our concern is this. The ultimate background of religious toleration in Virginia and that separation of Church and State in Virginia which is so important to the subject on the national level is not to be found in the pages of philosophers of the Enlightenment. It is not to be found in the comprehensive and creative imaginations of Thomas Jefferson and James Madison. The background is very much more prosaic, but very much more tangible. It is to be found in the fact that at last the Anglican Church in Virginia had in the western counties a rival potent enough to be a factor in every religious reckoning. Until the Great Awakening the minority in Virginia had been too small to make its viewpoint effective, and Virginia had the Established Church. After the Great Awakening the viewpoint of the minority was strong enough to bear effective weight, and it did. But that viewpoint always favored toleration, no matter what religious group comprised the minority in a given colony. The final and historic expression for Virginia of disestablishment and the separation of Church and State was to come from Jefferson and Madison. But the final motivation for disestablishment and the separation of Church and State in Virginia were supplied by the rivalry of Anglican and Presbyterian. As always, the roots were grounded in religion and not its opposite.

THE BAPTIST CONTRIBUTION

The greatest contribution of the Baptist phase of the Great Awakening to the twin ideals of toleration and the separation of Church and State lay in the strengthening of a church which was loyal to these ideals from the start. The English history of the Baptists starts with those religious liberals who moved successively from the Episcopal or Puritan position to the Baptist position, by way of Independency. With some, the movement ended there. With others, it continued into the Society of Friends or to that final haven of independence and individuality, the Seekers. The person who best epitomizes the chain of development is the man who tested in his own spiritual development its every link with the exception of the Quaker. He is Roger Williams.

As is well known and has been said repeatedly before, Roger Williams' Rhode Island became the New World haven for the discontented and the oppressed. Williams' own views on Church and State were so liberal and advanced that in his colony there was room for every church whose members would keep the general peace. Roger Williams was the prototype of the American ideal, but we would be taking too much credit to ourselves if we hailed Williams as literally the father of American toleration. It should, on the contrary, be soberly doubted if we of the twentieth century have as yet reached a position so advanced as that held by Roger Williams in the seventeenth.

The first pages of Baptist history in America still hold

their unsolved conundrums. It would seem that the first Baptist church was founded in America at Providence but that the first Baptist church was built at Newport, the former in 1639 and the latter in 1644, although Baptist services were held at Newport some years earlier. Baptists were to be found at Salem, Massachusetts, in 1642; an exodus of Lynn, Massachusetts, Baptists to Gravesend, Long Island, took place shortly after; and by 1651 there were enough Baptists in Massachusetts to pose a threat in orthodox minds. Fines were imposed, whippings took place, and in 1654 a figure no smaller than the president of Harvard College resigned his position after a squabble over infant baptism. The first Baptist church in Boston came into being in 1665, and it encountered the stormiest of waters until the Charter of 1691 granted "liberty of conscience to all Christians, except Papists." By 1718 the calm was halcyon, and two members of the Mather family participated in the ordination of a Baptist minister. The Baptist Church, however, still awaited the Great Awakening. By 1740 there were only twenty-two Baptist churches in New England, half of them in Rhode Island.

In the middle colonies and the South the Baptists did considerably better. The favorable atmosphere of Pennsylvania made Philadelphia the Baptist center for the New World by 1800. In Virginia the going was rougher for obvious reasons, and there were only three Baptist churches there in the middle of the eighteenth century. In the Carolinas, where Anglican opposition was less entrenched, the Baptists made better headway, but it remained for the later stages of the Great Awakening to give them the enormous growth which made the South what it is to this day, a Baptist stronghold. When the day of Awakening came, it brought with it an awakening to the Presbyterians as well. It has already been seen that the Presbyterians brought religious competition to the Virginia Anglicans, with the customary end result of toleration. The Separate Baptists, with an uneducated, unsalaried, and uninhibited ministry, brought revivalistic fervors beyond the Presbyterian ken, and what with whoopings and whinings, otherworldly disregard for licensing laws and other human ordainments, and an unabashed appeal to the unwashed, they seemed to Presbyterian eyes a menace as great as the Presbyterians seemed to the Anglicans. The customary arrests followed, along with the habitual mob scenes. But—also as usual—gradually the waters quieted. By 1770 the Separate Baptists of Virginia had come of emotional age and thereafter the growth of their Church was orderly and rapid. The old contempt in which the Presbyterians held them disappeared, the uncomprehending awe with which Tidewater Anglicans viewed them from afar passed away. Before the Revolution had entered history, there was a third great church solidly established in the Old Dominion.

Its presence was a further pledge that toleration and the separation of Church and State henceforth would be Virginia principles. Both ideals were enormously reinforced by the principles of the Baptists themselves. Without getting into the thorny question of the relationship between the Baptists and the Anabaptists of the continent, we have seen that toleration and the separation of Church and State had been Baptist principles from the start. Toleration and separation were inevitable in the South even by the juxtaposition of Anglicans and Presbyterians, who originally believed in neither. Toleration and separation were speeded by the addition of the Baptists, who believed in both. Add the burgeoning of Methodism, and the incorporation of the two principles into Virginian law became inevitable. The final honor of recognizing the inevitable is shared by Thomas Jefferson and James Madison.

9

State and Federal Constitutions

While the roads were long and rocky and the routes diverse and often strange, by the dawn of the American Revolution all the colonies were approaching or had reached a readiness to separate Church and State. Only Rhode Island had traveled no road and followed no route to reach that destination; Rhode Island had been there from the start. For Pennsylvania the route was short and direct; full civil rights had to be granted to Catholics and to disbelievers in the Trinity for full civil liberty to be achieved. In the other colonies, as has been seen, far reaching and profound changes in attitude were necessary before the modern concept could become a possibility.

The case of Virginia is of particular interest. The Church of England had been established there, and the establishment was stronger in Virginia than anywhere else. Then the Presbyterians won religious liberty for themselves against the opposition of the Episcopalians. Next the Baptists won religious liberty for themselves against the opposition of the Episcopalians and the Presbyterians. By 1775 about three quarters of the people of Virginia were outside the Church of England, but many of the most influential Virginians were inside. When the war started, there were ninety-five Anglican parishes in Virginia. The war killed off at least a quarter of them. Nowhere in the colonies was Tory sentiment stronger than among the Anglican clergy of Virginia, and they found themselves at the gravest of odds with their flocks. When the political test of establishment came, the establishment itself was torn by political dissension.

VIRGINIA'S BILL OF RIGHTS

The state convention met in 1776 for political purposes, but soon found itself at grips with a religious problem. From all over Virginia came petitions for the lifting of all restraints on freedom of conscience and worship. Presbyterians and Baptists in particular called for protection in their several forms of worship, exemption from taxes paid for the support of any church, and the repeal of all laws of establishment and religious preference. They were opposed by the Anglicans.

Section sixteen of the Virginia bill of rights, which concerns religion, was in the first instance the work of Patrick Henry. Dealing in a realistic fashion with the problem of religion in a commonwealth where the Established Church had lost its hold and rival churches of great strength were clamoring for their rights, he offered the following proviso: "That Religion, or the duty that we owe our Creator, and the manner of discharging it, can be directed only by reason and conviction, and not by force or violence; and, therefore [that all men should enjoy the fullest toleration in the exercise of religion according to the dictates of conscience, unpunished and unrestrained by the magistrate, unless under color of religion any man disturb the peace, the happiness, or safety of society; and], that it is the mutual duty of all to practice Christian forebearance, love, and charity towards each other."[1]

Madison objected to the portion bracketed above, arguing that toleration implies the presence of an established church to be tolerant. He proposed two amendments that were accepted:

> All men are equally entitled to the full and free exercise of religion according to the dictates of conscience.

> No man or class of men, ought on account of religion to be invested with peculiar emoluments or privileges, nor subjected to any penalties or disabilities, unless under color of religion the preservation of equal liberty and the existence of the State are manifestly endangered.

The process of disestablishment now gathered momentum. The legislature of 1776 exempted dissenters from taxes for the support of the Church. A subsequent act suspended the law fixing the salaries of clergymen, and the position of the Established Church was limited more and more rigidly by successive legislatures until the Declaratory Act of 1787 ended establishment in Virginia. The prime mover in the process was Thomas Jefferson, who describes in his *Autobiography* the length and bitterness of the struggle and expresses in memorable epigrams his own belief in full religious freedom.

The Established Church, however, did not give up without a struggle. In the later stages of disestablishment there was a curious alliance formed between the Episcopalian and the Presbyterian clergy with an eye to creating a new line of defense. In 1784 a bill was introduced "establishing a provision for teachers of the Christian religion." Buttressed by the influential support of George Washington, Patrick Henry, Richard Henry Lee, and John Marshall, it provided that the state should support the general diffusion of Christianity but without giving pre-eminence to any of the several sects. The effect of the measure would have been to make tax funds available for the support of the various churches, and the clergy of both the major Virginia churches were in favor of it. But the people were not, and Jefferson and Madison sensed the fact. Madison's *Memorial and Remonstrance,* which contended that religion did not come within the scope of government, had such overwhelming support from the people that the proposal was dropped.

In its place Jefferson and Madison presented their Declaratory Act, which became law in October 1785. After a philosophic preamble the act states: "Be it enacted by the General Assembly, That no man shall be compelled to frequent or support any religious worship, place, or ministry whatever; nor shall be enforced, restrained, molested, or burthened in his body or goods, nor shall otherwise suffer on account of his religious opinions or belief; but that all men shall be free to profess, and by argument to maintain, their opinion in matters of religion, and that the same shall in no wise diminish, enlarge, or affect their civil capacities."[2] Two years later the same principle of religious freedom was extended to the Northwest Territory by the Ordinance of 1787.

Thus religious toleration and the separation of Church and State in Virginia followed the growth of opposition to the Anglican establishment. Madison first and Jefferson shortly after put into legislation what the impact of events in Virginia had put into practice. The idea of establishment died hard, as the bill introduced in 1784 reveals. Those who were brought up in the tradition of the establishment and believed in its underlying principle fell back upon a second line of defense. They proposed what might be termed the establishment of Christianity, but without precedence in such an establishment to any particular church. Those who believe that the Founding Fathers were unanimously and totally opposed to the concept of establishment might ponder the fact that this proposal had the backing of George Washington, Patrick Henry, Richard Henry Lee, and John Marshall. But Thomas Jefferson and James Madison had the backing of the people of Virginia, and thus religious freedom in the broadest sense was triumphant.

One should note, however, precisely what comprised the separation of Church and State in the act of 1785. No one could be legally required to attend any church or support any ministry. No one could legally suffer any injury in his body or his goods because of his religious beliefs. All should be free to maintain their religious opinions, without benefit or loss from such professions of belief. In short, there were three factors in the equation: the Church, the State, and the Individual. The act of 1785 protected the individual from any loss at the hands of the State because of his relations to the Church. It did not attempt to define the relations between Church and State except in terms of the individual. It contained an implicit ban, of course, upon a church establishment, but beyond that it did not go. Efforts to read more into it inevitably take on the subjective cast of thought of the person who does the reading.

ENACTMENTS IN OTHER STATES

The legislative enactments of the other states require relatively little comment. In 1781 New Hampshire adopted a constitution which kept the Church as a tax-supported town institution and expressed itself in favor of the Protestant religion. In Massachusetts a similar situation prevailed as a result of the constitution of 1780. Bay State taxpayers were allowed to indicate the church to which they wished their tax payments to go, the taxes of those who did not indicate a preference going to the Congregational Church. Rhode Island and Connecticut did not adopt state constitutions. Full religious freedom continued to prevail in Rhode Island, but in Connecticut a system of tax allotment similar to that of Massachusetts and limited to the Protestant churches continued well into the nineteenth century. New York speedily wiped out the toehold which the Church of England held and reduced it to the same status as that of the other Christian churches; she first legislated against Catholics, then changed her mind and went the full way of Virginia. Pennsylvania at first assumed a position slightly less liberal than that of Virginia by limiting the civil rights of Catholics, but Benjamin Franklin later induced the legislature to remove such limitations. Delaware in 1776 granted citizenship to Trinitarian Christians. Maryland traveled the full road to religious freedom, although reserving for its legislature the right to levy taxes for the general support of Christianity, with the taxpayer indicating the ecclesiastical destination of his personal levy. North Carolina eliminated the old church establishment but limited officeholding to Protestants. South Carolina declared that the Christian Protestant religion was the established religion of the state, with all qualifying churches having equal rights and privileges. Georgia declared for religious freedom but limited membership in its legislature to Protestants.

In recapitulation, three states, Rhode Island, New York, and Virginia, granted full religious freedom. Three states, Pennsylvania, Delaware, and Maryland, demanded in different degrees adherence to Christianity. New Jersey, North Carolina, South Carolina, and Georgia demanded Protestantism. New Hampshire, Massachusetts, and Connecticut maintained their established Church.

The Constitutional Convention

In 1787 the Constitutional Convention faced the problem of finding a common denominator among these varying attitudes which ran the gamut from establishment to complete religious freedom, with all sorts of ideological way stations not indicated here. Some states, for example, demanded belief in the divine inspiration of the Bible; others demanded belief in heaven and hell. Three barred ministers from public office. One restricted liberty to Protestants and demanded active church membership. Another demanded belief in Trinitarian Christianity. Some provided tax revenues for the support of churches; others forbade this use of tax revenues. The very brevity of the religious clause of the First Amendment indicates how limited was the common denominator of agreement. It was agreed that Congress could not establish a church, that the newly created nation was to have no national church. Beyond that the framers of the Constitution could not go, even if they had a mind to go farther. An examination of the state constitutions speedily reveals why.

The historic view permits but one tenable interpretation of the First Amendment to the Constitution. It is not an interpretation in reality, but a literal reading. The first ten amendments, known collectively as the Bill of Rights, went into effect on November 3, 1791. The first article reads as follows: "Congress shall make no law respecting an establishment of religion, or prohibiting the free exercise thereof; or abridging the freedom of speech, or of the press; or the right of the people peaceably to assemble, and to petition the Government for a redress of grievances." It has been seen that the phrase "an establishment of religion" had a very definite eighteenth-century meaning. There had been an establishment of religion in Virginia and the other southern colonies for many decades. On the day that the Bill of Rights was passed, there was a quite different establishment of religion in New Hampshire, Massachusetts, and Connecticut. That establishment of the Congregational Church was to continue for many years. True, its days were numbered, but they were numbered by the spirit of the times and not by the letter of the Constitution. The Tenth Amendment protected the New England establishment quite adequately, the First Amendment did not prohibit it, and it is not a matter of record that the situation in New England elicited protest elsewhere or defense in the three states concerned. The established Church in New England simply existed as a matter of unchallenged fact, until the challenge came from within. The Tenth Amendment reads as follows: "The powers not delegated to the United States by the Constitution, nor prohibited by it to the States, are reserved to the States respectively, or to the people."

The failure of the framers of the Constitution to include a religious qualification for membership in Congress had not gone unchallenged in the Bay State. While the issue should not be ballooned out of proportion to the other and hotly contested issues in the great Federalist and anti-Federalist debate, several members of the Bay State delegation expressed grave disapproval of the omission, along with forebodings of its effect upon congressional morals. The genuine issue, the one which embraced all the others, was the first and most enduring issue in American politics, the issue of state rights. More guarantees of individual and state rights than the original draft contained were demanded from the start, and failure to meet such demands would have imperiled the Constitution. Madison proposed various additions to the document which were referred to committee. The committee reported seventeen amendments, of which twelve were ratified by the Senate and ten by all the states except

Massachusetts, Connecticut, and Georgia. These ten comprise the Bill of Rights.

It is essential to an understanding of the Bill of Rights to realize that its provisions were designed to limit the powers of the federal government but not of the state governments. In 1833 the Supreme Court held that the due-process clause of the Fifth Amendment could not be invoked against a city (*Barron* v. *Baltimore*, the city having interfered with a wharf owned by Barron). There is a constant tendency to lose the historic perspective in these matters. The Fourteenth Amendment has been held in the twentieth century to protect the individual against state encroachment on his religious liberties, but the Fourteenth Amendment was not proposed until seventy years after the adoption of the Bill of Rights. A 1946 Supreme Court decision (*Everson* v. *Board of Education*) stated, "The 'establishment of religion' clause of the First Amendment means at least this: Neither a state nor the Federal Government can set up a church. Neither can pass laws which aid one religion, aid all religions, or prefer one religion over another."

Actually, the First Amendment meant only a fraction of that when it was adopted. States did have established churches then; they did pass laws to aid one religion and to show preference for one religion over others long after the adoption of the First Amendment, and these facts went unchallenged for decades. When it was adopted, the First Amendment meant precisely what it said: Congress could make no law respecting an establishment of religion or prohibiting the free exercise thereof. The states were left free to deal with the problem of religion and religious establishments as they saw fit, under the provisions of their constitutions.

In our preoccupation with the phrase *establishment of religion*, we have tended to overlook the neutral force of the word *respecting*. The First Amendment forbade Congress to do anything, pro or con, about an establishment of religion. It could not impose one, but neither could it abolish one in a state where it already existed. As Justice Stewart put it in the Bible-reading case, "I accept too the proposition that the Fourteenth Amendment has somehow absorbed the establishment clause, although it is not without irony that a constitutional provision evidently designed to leave the states free to go their own way should now have become a restriction upon their autonomy."

There never was a time in American history when a national "wall of separation" was erected between Church and State by legislative fiat. The wall was slowly erected stone by stone, in some states earlier than in others, in some states more completely than in others. It is one of the curious anomalies of the recent history of the Supreme Court that a Court whose membership has shown a vigorous readiness to apply new viewpoints to certain ancient problems of society should view the American relationship of Church and State as if it had been from the beginning and was as the law of the Medes and the Persians, which altereth not.

10

Disestablishment in New England

Jefferson's phrase, "a wall of separation between Church and State," has been quoted so frequently, almost invariably with the connotation that the wall was complete on the day that the Bill of Rights was adopted, that the full words of Jefferson are worth repeating. Replying on January 1, 1802, to an address from a committee of the Danbury (Conn.) Baptist Association, Jefferson stated: "Believing with you that religion is a matter which lies solely between man and his God, that he owes account to none other for his faith or his worship, that the legislative powers of government reach actions only, and not opinions, I contemplate with sovereign reverence that act of the whole American people which declared that their legislature should 'make no law respecting an establishment of religion, or prohibiting the free exercise thereof,' thus building a wall of separation between Church and State. Adhering to this expression of the supreme will of the nation in behalf of the rights of conscience, I shall see with sincere satisfaction the progress of those sentiments

which tend to restore to man all his natural rights, convinced
he has no natural right in opposition to his social duties."[1]

That the wall was not complete the day that the Bill of
Rights was adopted is amply demonstrated by the state
constitutions of that date and many a date thereafter. The
truth is that the slow and often painful process of disestablishment proceeded for decades, especially in New England.
It would be manifestly absurd to suggest that either Thomas
Jefferson or the Baptist Association of Danbury, Connecticut,
a state with an established church, was unaware of the fact
nearly ten years after the Bill of Rights was adopted. Furthermore, the phrase "a wall of separation" is subject to all
the uncertainty which besets metaphors that are construed
literally. The reasonable assumption is that Jefferson saw
in the First Amendment to the Constitution the adoption,
at least on the national level, of the principle of separation
of Church and State. But a principle is not a wall, metaphor-
ically speaking or literally speaking.

It is of further interest to observe that Jefferson in 1801
was still thinking in terms of the equation with three factors,
the Church, the State, and the Individual, which underlay
the Virginia Act of 1785. He thought of religion as a direct
concern between man and God, he believed that man owed
religious allegiance to no earthly power, that the control of
an individual's thoughts and beliefs was beyond the power of
the state, and that the passage of the First Amendment was
a forward step in "the progress of those sentiments which
tend to restore to man all his natural rights." This makes
obvious historic sense and is a good projection of what was
to come in America's future. Furthermore, Jefferson's primary concern obviously was the individual and his rights.
The purpose of the First Amendment, as Jefferson's communication to the Danbury Baptists makes clear, was to
protect the individual in the exercise of his religious rights.
There was nothing in it to define the relations of Church

and State, except in terms of the individual and in terms of its explicit prohibition of a congressionally established church. Eighteenth-century liberals, unlike many of the twentieth century, always thought first in terms of the individual and his rights.

SLOW PROGRESS

Thomas Jefferson thought in such terms in 1801, but the sons of Calvin who still held forth in three of the five New England states thought otherwise. In what follows it is well to remember that Maine was part of Massachusetts until 1820, that Vermont became a state in 1791 but that it was split ideologically between New Hampshire and New York, which had contested it politically, and that Rhode Island in its religious history is unique among the states. The slow progress of New England toward disestablishment is to be observed in three states, Massachusetts, Connecticut, and New Hampshire.

In 1711 residents of Boston were exempted from compulsory taxation for the support of the Church. As time passed, the same principle of voluntary contribution was extended to other communities. But the extension was gradual, and it was far from complete by the outbreak of the Revolution. The real test of the Bay State attitude toward religion came when the hour for a state constitution arrived. The proposed constitution of 1778 contained two clauses comparable to the ones adopted in certain states of the South. They read as follows:

> XXIX. No person unless of the Protestant Religion shall be Governor, Lieutenant Governor, a member of the Senate or of the House of Representatives or hold any judiciary employment within this state.

XXXIV. The free exercise and enjoyment of religious profession and worship shall forever be allowed to every denomination of Protestants within this State.[2]

The liberals of Boston, for such they were contrasted with
the stalwarts of the hinterland, rose in protest. By their side
rose the people of Essex County, under the redoubtable
Theophilus Parsons. They won, and the constitution of 1778
was rejected. More would be heard in American politics of
the Essex Junto.

The limited measure of their victory, however, is to be
found in the actual provisions of the constitution adopted.
Article II guaranteed freedom of conscience in terms that
would have been acceptable to Madison and Jefferson. But
Article III proceeded to set up something very close to a
full religious establishment. By it the legislature was authorized and directed to require "the several parishes, precincts,
and other bodies politic, or religious societies" to institute
public worship and support "public protestant teachers of
piety, religion, and morality, in all cases, where such provisions shall not be made voluntarily."[3] The legislature was
authorized to require attendance at religious services; the
towns and other bodies politic would have the right to elect
their religious teachers and to contract for their support; the
individual might designate the church to which his taxes
would go if there was one of his denomination in the community; but otherwise it would go "toward the support of the
teacher, or teachers of the parish, or precinct in which said
moneys are raised."[4]

The article concludes with a round declaration of religious
equality: "And every denomination of Christians, demeaning themselves peaceably, and as good subjects of the Commonwealth, shall be equally under the protection of the law;
and no subordination of any sect or denomination to another
shall ever be established by law." However, the spirit of

this declaration of religious equality, if not the full letter, was nullified by the oath of office which required the abjuration of "any jurisdiction, superiority, pre-eminence, authority, dispensing or other power, in any matter civil ecclesiastical or spiritual within this commonwealth. . . ."[5] This would effectively rule out Anglicans, of whom at least Boston had by now its share, and any hypothetical Catholics who might be elevated toward public office by their Calvinistic fellow citizens.

SEMI-ESTABLISHMENT IN MASSACHUSETTS

An objective examination of the Massachusetts constitution shows that what might be termed a semi-establishment was brought into being. The legislature had no authority over doctrine. The taxes of a Baptist, Episcopalian, Methodist, or Universalist might go to his own church if he had a church near enough to attend. There was nothing like the established Church of Puritan days. There was, however, a compromise between the old concept of establishment and the new concept of disestablishment which left the Congregational Church in a favored position. The issue was debated with that peculiar intensity which characterizes the New England town meeting, and the records of debate, with the smoke of battle not yet entirely drifted away, are to be found in New England archives. The constitution triumphed by a vote of 5654 to 2047, but the record of dissent to the religious provisions that is to be found in these archives suggests that Article III might have fared worse than the document as a whole if acceptance or rejection had been article by article.

Article III soon showed itself a religious Pandora's box. Dissenters from the Congregational Church had to file certificates of dissent. What this did to the provision that "no subordination of any sect or denomination to another shall ever be established by law" was the not unreasonable question of the Baptists and Universalists. On one occasion the tax funds of a Universalist minister were contested by the state on the grounds that a clergyman "who denied the eternal punishment of the wicked was not a teacher of 'piety, religion and morality.'"[6] The court deemed otherwise.

The really serious problem, however, was presented by the intangible yet potent factor, the atmosphere of a state where the ruling and official class belonged to the Congregational Church and the place yielded to others was scant and grudging. The power of that Church was the greater for the close co-operation between its spiritual leaders and the dominant political forces in the Commonwealth; the Boston clergy was active in the fight over Jay's Treaty and in the promotion of the Federalist cause. In 1797 the clerical-Federalist alliance in Massachusetts found a court which would rule that "a man's being ordained over a voluntary association, formed by no act of government, and bound by no law, could not be a settled minister within the meaning of the act."[7] The peril that this ruling presented to ministers dissenting from Congregationalism was obvious, nor was it dispelled until the passage of the Religious Freedom Bill of 1811.

About the turn of the century, the center of conservatism shifted from Boston to the western part of the state. This marked a reversal of the situation which had existed previously, and it was the result of two quite different causes. In Boston and the rest of eastern Massachusetts, the rise of Unitarianism and the influx of immigrants began to dilute what had been the concentrated Congregationalism. But in the Connecticut Valley and the Berkshire country a shift in population was taking place. The malcontents of Shays's Rebellion were moving out into the wilds of Vermont or the far more fertile state of New York. Their place was being taken by the sturdiest of Congregationalists, who moved up the valley from Connecticut bringing Federalist majorities with them. Jeffersonian democracy might win the day elsewhere in the United States, but Federalist doctrine and the theology that was its natural ally became so firmly entrenched in western Massachusetts that the signs of their presence are far from obliterated even today.

As time passed, the nature of the semi-establishment in Massachusetts was more closely defined by a series of court cases. It was decided that a town could not collect church taxes for any purpose other than the building of a church and the support of its ministers. It was decided that the vote to call or dismiss a minister was open to all voters of a town or parish and not restricted, as in colonial days, to the covenanted members of the congregation. The Baptists and Methodists kept battling away for their full religious rights, the Baptists being particularly vigorous in the fight against compulsory worship and compulsory church taxes. Just as the instinct of the Congregational Church led it to support the Federalist Party, so the Baptist instinct put in on the side of the Republican, or Jeffersonian, Party. The Baptists found natural allies in the Methodists, and on occasion the Episcopalians found it possible to submerge theological differences in a common cause.

The growing strength of the ecclesiastical opposition tended to tighten Congregational ranks. A Federalist victory in 1810 expedited a court finding that church taxes could go only to ministers presiding over incorporated societies, and Federalist legislatures showed considerable reluctance to give papers of incorporation to conventicles of the dissenting sects. The next year, however, the political tide turned, and with it the religious tide. The Republicans went into office and passed the Religious Freedom Act of 1811, which wiped out the effects of the court decisions mentioned and denied public officials the right to supervise religious instruction.

THE TIDE TURNED

The tide had turned, but the current was still vague and uncertain. Only the Unitarian schism in the Congregational Church kept the 1811 act on the books in 1812 when the Federalists won at the polls. But doom was at hand for the Federalist cause. Its opposition to the national policy in the War of 1812 speeded it into the pages of history, and thereafter the Federalists ceased to be a national party and became a political vestigial remains, active only in New England. Again the courts became an important factor in Bay State theology. A ruling that the towns and not the churches had the right to elect the minister led to a steady transfer of church property. The Congregational Church was split down the middle, or more accurately to the left of the middle, by the Unitarian controversy. Gradually the Unitarians came to outnumber the Trinitarians. When an election took place, the church property would pass to the Unitarians and the Trinitarians would have to form a new Congregational church. Loud laments from the conservative faithful did not slow down a process which changed the theology expounded in $608,000 worth of church property, according to one contemporary theologico-economic jeremiad.

But again, the inexorable processes which made for disestablishment did not proceed without interruption. At the Constitutional Convention of 1820 the Trinitarians and the Unitarians found it possible to effect a truce while they fought for compulsory church attendance against a united front of Baptists, Methodists, Quakers, and Universalists. It did not escape the notice of the conservatively devout that one tangible result of the system of filing a certificate of dissent was often a late Sunday sleep by the unrighteous. There is also the black sheep reported by Samuel Hoar who strayed from the Congregational fold, was immersed by the Baptists, conceded that his sins perhaps had not been washed away, but stoutly maintained that his taxes had. The conservative forces held the field when the votes were counted. The oath of office was amended to a short form with no theological overtones, but the proposals to delete the word *Protestant* from the state bill of rights and to give a constitutional guarantee to the Religious Freedom Bill of 1811 were easily defeated. Daniel Webster mourned, "The sects in this country . . . required . . . more guards against the oppression of each other, than they would in Turkey against the oppression of the Grand Seignior." The meeting-house clocks of Massachusetts had not moved between 1780 and 1820.

They were soon to move and in the moving to strike a new hour. The Federalist Party was perilously close to its last stand in 1820. The less affluent were steadily growing in strength, and even western Massachusetts began to change its political and religious complexion as Baptist and Methodist infiltrations set in from New York. In 1823 Harrison Gray Otis went down to defeat in a statewide election before his Republican opponent. The Reverend Lyman Beecher of Boston read the handwriting on the political wall with crystal clarity: "The numerical, and political, and secular influence of the evangelical population is becoming powerful in this city, compelling Unitarian ambition to show less contempt and more courtesy to the orthodox. The late election has broken, and will, in its consequences, break forever their power as a Unitarian political party to proselyte, and annoy, and defend by perverted legislative and judicial influence. This, at least, is the opinion here. They feel their downfall."[8]

The Republicans at once facilitated the formation and recognition of religious societies separated from the regular parishes. Conservative Congregationalists preferred to send their sons to Baptist Brown, not to godless, alias Unitarian, Harvard. Industrialists began to build cotton mills on Massachusetts streams and Irish immigration by 1830 was providing a new element in the population, disturbing to the Calvinists but intriguing to the politicians. The Transcendental Movement brought new, disturbing, and yeasty ideas to such Unitarian minds as were open to them. Here and there a town cried a plague on both your houses and went Universalist. Varied as these factors were, they had a common denominator, the spirit of change. The One-Hoss Shay of the Yankee allegory was collapsing in the dust. In 1831 the House of Representatives voted disestablishment, 272 to 78, and also voted to annul Article III. The more conservative Senate voted otherwise and reaffirmed its opposition in 1832. But the temper of the Bay State was aroused, and the Senate bowed to the gathering storm. The issue was presented to the people, and on November 11, 1833, in the ratio of ten to one, the people swept Article III into oblivion and with it the last vestige of the old Puritan establishment. The new Article substituted for it read: "As the public worship of God, and instructions in piety, religion, and morality, promote the happiness and prosperity of a people, and the security of a republican government; therefore, the several religious societies of this Commonwealth, whether corporate or unincorporate, at any meeting legally warned and holden for that purpose shall ever have the right to elect their pastors or religious teachers, to contract with them for their support, to raise money for erecting and repairing houses for public worship, for the maintenance of religious instruction, and for the payment of necessary expenses; and all persons belonging to any religious society shall be taken and held to be members, until they shall file with the clerk of such society a written notice declaring the dissolution of their membership, and thenceforth shall not be liable for any grant or contract which may be thereafter made or entered into by such society: And all religious sects and denominations demeaning themselves peaceably, and as good citizens of the Commonwealth, shall be equally under the protection of the law; and no subordination of any one sect or denomination to another shall ever be established by law."[9]

With these words the last vestige of the Puritan Church-State was swept from the Massachusetts scene. It had endured for 203 years, if one dates its existence from the founding of Boston. At its zenith it had been as absolute a theocracy as the Christian world has ever known. Its powers of survival, however shorn of their full strength, were tremendous. Its mark upon American life, far more of it for good than is always conceded although more of it for bad than its apologists confess, has been profound. It may well be questioned if any single factor, with the exception of the frontier spirit of the South and West, has done as much to make America what it is as has the Puritanism of New England. It took forty-two years for the wall of separation between Church and State to be erected in Massachusetts, dating the laying of the first brick from the passage of the First Amendment to the Constitution of the United States. As always and everywhere in this country, it was the massive force of religious divergence and competition which finally made inevitable that separation in Massachusetts. It came later in the Bay State than in the other states outside New England because the Congregational Church was more firmly entrenched there than was any other church in any other state. Article XI, quoted above, replaced the discredited Article III. It should be noted, however, that Article XI is couched fully in the vocabulary of religion and is motivated as fundamentally by the spirit of religion as the article it replaced. Church and State were separated in Massachusetts, as always and everywhere in the United States, in the name of religion and not in the name of secularism.

STRUGGLE IN CONNECTICUT

Boston was not the only New World Geneva in the high noon of Puritanism. Connecticut was dotted with its replicas in miniature of the Calvinist stronghold, and the phrase *in miniature* ceases to be appropriate when one reaches New Haven. Connecticut had its law of 1698 which required every town to provide by taxation for its minister. It had its act of 1708, which provided that the churches of the state be united in doctrine, worship, and discipline under the principles accepted by the Congregational synod at Saybrook. Provision was made for separate worship by those who soberly differed or dissented from the established church, but they had to pay the Congregational Church tax even as did the orthodox faithful. Pay it they did until May 1777, when an act exempting them on the filing of certificates was passed. In 1784 the laws were revised, and it was deemed right to drop the 1708 statute with its explicit recognition of the established church.

The act of 1708 was dropped from the statutes, but the reality which it recognized did not drop from Connecticut life. Dissenters still had to file their certificates, and town taxes still were applied to the support of the Congregational Church with the exception of the levies on those who explicitly directed otherwise. To the sons of Calvin in the line royal this seemed the utmost in liberality, but the dissenters from Congregationalism deemed otherwise. The Baptists, as always, were foremost in their opposition. One John Leland pointed out how far short the statutes of 1784 fell of the ideal of entire religious liberty: "The certificate that a dissenter produces to the society-clerk, must be signed by some officer of the dissenting church, and such church must be protestant-christian; for heathens, deists, Jews, and papists are not indulged in the certificate law; all of them, as well as Turks, must therefore be taxed to the standing order, though they never go among them or know where the meeting-house is."[10]

The reply of the Standing Order was to require two additional signatures on the dissenter's certificate. Conciliation was never a major Calvinist achievement.

Ten years passed, and the May assembly of 1794 found the Baptists storming the State House at Hartford. The lower house recognized *force majeure* and beat a legislative retreat marked by speed rather than grace. The council stood its ground, and the net gain from the attack was in an area far removed from the battlefield: a concession was made whereby the Western Lands Bill was given a public school fund proviso. During the closing years of the century the battle lines in Connecticut were the same as in Massachusetts. An orthodox Congregationalist was also a Federalist, a dissenter from Congregationalism was a Republican. Even the Episcopalians, with personal backgrounds that would incline them toward the Federalist Party if religious interests did not tug in the opposite direction, were to be found mainly in the Republican camp. The refusal of the legislature to grant the Episcopalians a charter for a college in Connecticut was for many the decisive factor.

The Federalist rout on the national scene in 1816 had its Connecticut repercussions. The general assembly attempted some very fancy division of the spoils from the general defense fund due to the state by the federal government. In an edifying display of religious fervor, the assembly decided that in the main the spoils should go to the churches. The minority religious groups found less edifying a division which gave one third to the Congregational Church and one seventh to Yale, reserving one seventh for the Episcopalians, one eighth for the Baptists, one twelfth for the Methodists, and one sixth for the state treasury. The heathens, deists,

Jews, and papists did not participate, nor did the Turks. For two years the Methodists refused to accept their assigned share, and when they did it was over the protest of many of their members. The Baptists held out until 1820.

The forces of disestablishment took a major step forward in 1818. In the crucial Article VII of the revised state constitution there was provided a complete severance of Church and State, a constitutional guarantee of the right to freedom of conscience, and a guarantee of complete equality before the law of all Christian bodies. The last proviso would make the battle seem far from won. The real point at issue in 1818 did not concern the next to hypothetical heathens, Jews, papists, and Turks previously mentioned. It concerned the very real and numerically far from negligible Unitarians and Universalists whose churches, in the theological judgment of the Connecticut assembly, did not qualify as Christian bodies. The good men and true of Hartford saw what was happening to Congregationalism around Boston, and they had no stomach for it. The battle, however, really was over even if many of the warriors did not realize it. State support was withdrawn from the Congregational Church by the revised constitution of 1818, but today the chastely proportioned lines of many a white church in many a Connecticut town prove that Congregationalism survived. The stigma of the certificate, which carried social and economic overtones as well as theological, was removed from the dissenters, and Connecticut moved forward in the direction of democratic equality. Even those who shook their heads in foreboding came to see their fears unrealized. Lyman Beecher's first verdict was, "as dark a day as I ever saw." Later he revised his view to, "the best thing that ever happened to the State of Connecticut." In a way unrecorded but presumably by time's imperceptible osmosis, Unitarians and Universalists came to be regarded as Christians, with

all the rights and privileges appertaining to that status. Today in Connecticut, living in religious peace and freedom,
are Jews, papists, and Turks. And the Nutmeg State also
has its heathens.

The Granite of New Hampshire

Those who believe that the First Amendment to the Constitution erected a wall of separation between Church and
State in every state should find the case of New Hampshire
instructive. The first provincial assembly met at Portsmouth
in 1680. It ordained that all English Protestants twenty-
four years of age, "not viceous in life but of honest and good
conversation, and such as have £20 Ratable estate" were
freemen and had the right to vote.[11] It took nearly 250 years
for the final echo of that decision to die away under the
Granite State's miniature dome at Concord.

The Congregational Church was established in New
Hampshire, in the fashion made familiar by the procedure
in Massachusetts and Connecticut, by laws enacted in 1692,
1702, and 1714. The freeholders of the town engaged the
minister and contracted with him for his salary, which the
selectmen proceeded to assess and the constable to collect.
A dissenter from Congregationalism was exempted from his
church tax only upon proving his regular attendance at another Protestant church and his steady support of it—and
provincial New Hampshire town officials were not easily
convinced.

When the day came for the writing of a state constitution,
the lawmakers of New Hampshire vied in eloquence with
their compeers in southern New England in expressing the
fervor of their devotion to the ideal of religious toleration.
Then, in a way already familiar from a reading of the Massachusetts and Connecticut record, they proceeded to limit

the governorship and membership in either house of the legislature to Protestants. A series of valiant efforts was made by the foremost battler for religious freedom in New Hampshire history, William Plumer, to strike out this sectarian requirement. He failed utterly, and the requirement that the state's chief elected officers be Protestants is to be found in the constitution of 1783. Articles IV–VI of the New Hampshire constitution so closely parallel Articles II and III of the Massachusetts constitution as to make verbal as well as ideological plagiarism suspect.

The customary battle of the sects set in when the practical problem of collecting church taxes arose. The assumption in New Hampshire, as in Connecticut, was that a person was a Congregationalist unless he furnished overpowering proof to the contrary. If he was an Episcopalian, he usually fared all right. If he was a Baptist, a Methodist, or a Universalist, the odds were hopelessly against him. These creeds were not of sufficient numerical strength in so thinly populated a state to support many churches. Consequently their members had a Hobson's choice. They could pay taxes to the Congregational Church, which they never attended and in the dogmas of which they had no belief, or they could languish in one of New Hampshire's less than commodious local jails.

The first crack in the granite appeared in 1804. New Hampshire was far from the main political battlefields, but battles won elsewhere were not without their New Hampshire effects. In 1800 Thomas Jefferson was elected in a Republican triumph over the Federalists. This implied, among other things, a victory for religious toleration, since the election of 1800 was in a sense a referendum on the issue of the State Church. The Baptists were the first to benefit by the change in atmosphere, although it took four years for the freshening breeze to reach New Hampshire. On December 7, 1804, the Baptists were recognized by the New

Hampshire legislature in the following resolution: "Re-solved, that the people of this state, commonly known by the name of the Free-will Anti-Pedo Baptists church and society shall be considered as a distinct religious sect or denomination, with all the privileges as such, agreeably to the Constitution."[12] In 1805 the Universalists gained recog-nition, and in 1807, the Methodists. Religious attendance, of course, remained upon a compulsory basis, but the mem-bers of the three newly recognized churches could incorpo-rate as separate religious societies.

Across the Connecticut River meanwhile, in the hitherto unmentioned state of Vermont, omens and portents were to be observed. Vermont, in the days before its birth as a state, had been a dark and bloody ground, hotly contested by New Hampshire and New York. There was something of the spirit of each of the rivals in its makeup, and something that was added by the radicals of Shays's Rebellion, who sought refuge in its fastnesses in their hour of defeat. There was, besides, something of the spirit of individual freedom that has been, is, and ever shall be native to Vermont. Until 1791, when Vermont broke away from New Hampshire, it had the same church legislation. In 1801 the certificate sys-tem for dissenters was considerably liberalized. Vermonters were not satisfied with halfway measures. In 1807 the One-Hoss Shay, ill-adapted to the dirt roads of Vermont, fell apart. Towns were forbidden to build churches and support ministers by levying taxes, and religion was placed on an entirely voluntary basis. It took sixteen years to erect the wall of separation in Vermont; by 1807 Vermont had taken its place beside Rhode Island as the home of religious tolera-tion in New England. The record of the struggle for religious toleration in the Green Mountain State is a short one marked by steady success, and it is entirely honorable to the name of Vermont.

In New Hampshire the letter of the law, at least, lingered

over a century behind Vermont's example. At first, progress in the direction of toleration was encouragingly rapid. Through the years the leading New Hampshire proponent of toleration, William Plumer, kept up the good fight, waging it on occasion from the vantage point of the state house. Elected governor in 1812, he was defeated in the next three successive elections, which then were annual, but was returned to office in 1816 and again in 1817. In 1816 a bill was filed with the legislature to repeal the establishment of the Congregational Church in the towns of New Hampshire and to annul the provision that Congregational ministers be supported by general taxation. A substitute measure filed by the Reverend Dan Young, Methodist minister of Lisbon, provided that ". . . all persons voluntarily associating to build a house of worship, or hire a minister of the Gospel, should be held to the fulfillment of their contract, but no person should be compelled to go into such a contract."[13]

In 1816 this measure received exactly four votes. One year later it received half the votes of the New Hampshire senate. In 1818 it swept the senate but was stalled by a tie vote in the house. In 1819 again it swept the senate and despite a desperate last ditch stand by the faithful, it carried the house. The Toleration Act of 1819 guaranteed to Protestant dissenters from Congregationalism the right to incorporate their religious societies. It made no provisions for non-Protestants, Christian or otherwise. The requirement that public officials be Protestants remained unchanged. In short, it did the minimum. Sufficient opposition to Congregationalism had arisen through the ranks of the Baptists, Methodists, Unitarians, and Universalists to guarantee these dissenting Protestant groups their rights. No comparable pressure had arisen from any other source, and so no toleration was extended in any other direction.

Decades passed. America changed, and even New Hampshire changed, but the New Hampshire constitution did not change. During these decades Catholics were appearing in New Hampshire in increasing numbers, some of them Irish moving up from Massachusetts, some of them French moving down from Quebec. By 1850 Catholic pressure had risen to the point of meriting the attention of astute politicians, Franklin Pierce among them. After due consideration of the menace to American institutions represented by the Pope at Rome, the delegates to the 1850 constitutional convention girded about them the bright sword of liberalism, dropped the word *Protestant* from the state bill of rights, extended legal protection to those of religions other than Christian, and dropped the religious requirements from the qualifications for state office. The proposed amendments to the bill of rights and the proposed elimination of the religious test for state office then were submitted to the electorate. The amendments to the bill of rights were rejected by a vote of 25,014 to 15,738. The elimination of the religious test was rejected by a vote of 25,670 to 13,836.

There the matter rested until 1876. In that year another constitutional convention was called, and again the issue of eliminating the word *Protestant* from the bill of rights and striking out the religious test for state officeholders was raised. This time the resolution was beaten in the convention itself. Second thought prevailed, however, and again the issue was extended to the electorate. The results of the balloting are interesting, partly as reflecting a change in the temper of the times and partly as indicative of the effect of the following referendum question: "Do you approve the proposed amendment, prohibiting money raised by taxation from being applied to the support of the schools or institutions of any religious sect or denomination as proposed in the amended Constitution?" This represented, of course, a quid pro quo. A vote to eliminate the religious test for state office and to expunge the word *Protestant* from the bill of rights might be accompanied by a vote to deny any tax money to Catholic schools or other Catholic institutions. On the basis of that compromise the religious test was abolished by a vote of 28,477 to 14,231. The word *Protestant*, however, remained in the bill of rights. The necessary two-thirds vote was not obtained, although the margin of failure was slight. The vote was 27,664 to 15,907. The denial of tax support to religious schools and institutions swept through by a vote of 35,838 to 6606.

VESTIGIAL REMAINS

As the nineteenth century drew to a close, there was left in the constitution of New Hampshire two last vestigial remains from the days of religious establishment. They were the phrases in the bill of rights, *evangelical principles* and *public Protestant teachers of piety, religion, and morality*. And yet, these verbal echoes from centuries gone by still spoke with meaning in the Granite State to those with ears attuned to what they said. When the next constitutional convention was assembled in 1889, their elimination was proposed. But 1889 was a poor year in which to propose in granite-ribbed areas the excision even of the vestigial remains of Calvinism. The convention itself showed a willingness, but when the proposal to make the bill of rights nonsectarian was presented to the electorate, it fell short of the necessary two-thirds majority. Actually the cause of religious liberalism had lost substantial ground since 1877, when the resolutions of the 1876 convention had been presented to the electorate. In 1877 the vote to eliminate the word *Protestant* from the bill of rights barely failed to receive the necessary two-thirds majority. In 1889 it failed by a thumping margin, 27,737 voting Yes and 20,048 voting No.

Thirteen years later found the clock still stopped. The constitutional convention of 1902 proposed the substitution of *Christian* for *evangelical,* and the elimination of *Protestant* from the beleaguered bill of rights. The electorate would have none of it. Not only was the necessary two-thirds majority not approached, but the forces of religious reaction nearly matched in numbers the enlightened. The vote was 16,611 to 15,727. Nor was the situation different in 1912. The line still held, the vote being 16,555 to 14,315. Nor did woman suffrage make a difference, except the usual difference of doubling the vote.

In 1922 the New Hampshire electorate was asked: "Do you approve of amending the Bill of Rights by striking out the words 'rightly grounded on evangelical principles' after the words 'As morality and piety' and striking out the word 'Protestant' before the words 'teachers of piety, religion and morality,' as proposed in the amendment to the Constitution?" This time reaction came out in front. The vote was 37,100 in the affirmative and 44,750 in the negative. In 1877, 64 per cent of the New Hampshire electorate had favored the elimination of the word *Protestant* from the state bill of rights; in 1922, 45 per cent favored its elimination. The case of New Hampshire offers cold comfort to the theorist who believes that the First Amendment to the Constitution of the United States built a wall of separation between Church and State. It may well be questioned if the New Hampshire sector of that wall was quite so high in 1922 as it had been in 1877.

There the matter rests to this day. The New Hampshire bill of rights still refers to "morality and piety, rightly grounded on evangelical principles." The only groups specifically stated to be "equally under the protection of the law" in New Hampshire are "every denomination of Christians." While the Granite State legislature shows no inclination to act upon it, it still has the legal power "to authorize, from time to time, the several towns, parishes, bodies corporate, or religious societies, within this state, to make adequate provision, at their own expense, for the support and maintenance of public Protestant teachers of piety, religion, and morality . . ." The historic connotation of the word *teacher* implies, of course, preacher or clergyman, and has no connection with the modern meaning, classroom instructor.

Such are the last vestigial remains of New England Calvinism. They are archaic survivals and of no present consequence. They are not, however, accidental survivals. They survive because the New Hampshire electorate as recently as 1922 voted survival for them. Insofar as the voting record shows, as recently as one generation ago the voters of New Hampshire refused to recognize as valid in their state the philosophy of the separation of Church and State expressed in the First Amendment to the Constitution of the United States.

11

Disestablishment outside New England

Outside New England the fight for disestablishment and
full religious rights was less hotly contested and more easily
won. But this is not to say that a battle was not necessary. It
will be recalled that of the original states only Rhode Island
and Virginia had full religious freedom at the start of state-
hood. New York had religious freedom that was close to
complete. The Empire State required the foreign-born, as
a prerequisite to naturalization, to abjure foreign ecclesiastical authority. This requirement was obviously aimed at
Catholics. It survived until 1806, when it was abolished so
that a Catholic, Francis Cooper, might take the assembly
seat to which he had been elected.

In neighboring New Jersey until 1844 a Catholic could
not hold elective office, although there were no restrictions
on Catholics as voters. The nineteenth article of the New
Jersey constitution of 1776 provided: "That there shall be
no establishment of any one religious sect in this Province,
in preference to another; and that no Protestant inhabitant
of this Colony shall be denied the enjoyment of any civil

right, merely on account of his religious principles; but that all persons, professing a belief in the faith of any Protestant sect, who shall demean themselves peaceably under the government, as hereby established, shall be capable of being elected into any office of profit or trust, or being a member of either branch of the Legislature, and shall fully and freely enjoy every privilege and immunity enjoyed by others their fellow subjects."[1]

With verbal changes appropriate to the subsequent status of New Jersey in the Union, this remained the basic law for sixty-six years. In 1844 the New Jersey constitution was amended to remove this civil disability from Catholic and other non-Protestant citizens of the state. The article quoted was then revised to read: "There shall be no establishment of one religious sect in preference to another; no religious test shall ever be required for any office or public trust; and no person shall be denied the enjoyment of any civil right merely on account of his religious principles."[2]

In Pennsylvania, which had from the start an enlightened attitude toward religious freedom, the one restrictive clause in the constitution of 1776 limited in practice the civil rights of Jews. The following oath was provided for those elected to the legislature: "I do believe in one God, the creator and governor of the universe, the rewarder of the good and punisher of the wicked. And I do acknowledge the Scriptures of the Old and New Testament to be given by Divine inspiration."[3] The next clause forbade any further religious test for office. A charitable attitude is in order toward the pious framers of this oath of office; when the Jews of Philadelphia petitioned that the requirement to subscribe to the New Testament be dropped, the entirely reasonable nature of their request was recognized. In 1790 the oath was rephrased to permit a Jew elected to office to attest to his fundamental religious belief without doing violence to his specific creed. As reworded, the law read: "That no person, who acknowledges the being of a God and a future state of rewards and punishments, shall, on account of his religious sentiments, be disqualified to hold any office or place of trust or profit under this commonwealth."[4] Secularism has made no progress toward modifying the fundamentally religious spirit of Pennsylvania law. The statute of 1790 still stands among the laws of Pennsylvania.

THE "JEW BILL" OF MARYLAND

In Maryland, on the other hand, the struggle for the full civil rights of Jews was protracted and bitter. The unique religious history of Maryland will be recalled. Originally founded under Catholic auspices, Maryland at first provided full religious freedom. But the bulk of the Maryland population was never Catholic. As has already been seen, control passed from the hands of the Catholic Calverts into the hands of the Puritans, and this resulted in a speedy but transient attempt to set up the Calvinistic Church-State. As the political complexion of the mother country changed, the complexion of Maryland changed with it. By 1715 the Calverts were safely Episcopalian, and the Church of England had been established in the colony even before the colony was restored to Calvert control. The constitution of 1776 disestablished the Church of England, but provided what was in effect an establishment of Christianity in its place. The document authorized the legislature to lay "a general and equal tax, for the support of the Christian religion," and a "declaration of a belief in the Christian religion" was required for "any office of trust or profit" in the state.[5]

One effort and one only was made to enforce this tax. The effort was made in 1785 and was defeated. The law, however, effectively barred Jews from public office in Maryland, and the bars stayed up until 1826.

The first attempt to remove the disability was made in 1797. A petition was addressed to the legislature which received favorable recognition in committee but no legislative action. The same fate befell petitions in 1801 and 1803. In 1810 the law which permitted the levying of a church tax was repealed, but no action was taken on the matter of the civil rights of Jews.

In 1818 a native of Paisley, Scotland, named Thomas Kennedy took up the battle for Jewish rights. It was a matter of sheer devotion to an American principle that inspired this adopted son of Maryland. He told the House of Delegates that "he had not the slightest acquaintance with any Jews in the world," nor is this surprising. It has been estimated that there were hardly more than one hundred Jews in Maryland at that time.[6] But Kennedy had his gleam to follow, and he followed it for eight difficult and weary years. In 1819 he introduced legislation to remove the Jewish civil disabilities. He was defeated. He reintroduced it in 1820. The vote of the legislature proved that he had gained no ground. He pleaded for his viewpoint with all the spread-eagle eloquence of the early nineteenth century, and found his fellow Mainliners holding the line. He burst into verse, rhyming couplet upon rhyming couplet, and found it had no charms to soothe the breast of Maryland. His campaign for re-election, indeed, was hampered by one of the first outbursts of anti-Semitism in American politics. He was re-elected and again presented his measure, which in 1822 was passed by the legislature. Maryland law, however, required that it be adopted by the next legislature as well, before it might become the law of the state. The second time it was defeated.

In 1826 the "Jew bill," as it was popularly known, finally passed the legislative hurdle. The same year the 65,000 people of Baltimore elected two members of the city's Jewish population, which hardly numbered two hundred by this date, to the city council. Their election was in part a recognition of personal qualities in the men, Solomon Etting and Jacob I. Cohen, and in part an act of atonement. Among the more pleasant aspects of the fight over the Jew bill was the loyalty of Maryland Catholics to the principles of religious freedom which characterized their initial control of the Maryland province. Their numbers were insufficient to be effective in the legislative voting, and the ultimate passage of the bill depended on winning the good will and tolerance of the Protestant members, but Cohen paid full tribute to the warmth of Catholic support and the entire absence of any Catholic opposition to Kennedy's measure in 1819, when support was scant and opposition powerful.[7] Kennedy did not live long after the hour of victory. In 1832 Maryland was swept by the Asiatic cholera, and Thomas Kennedy was among the victims.

DISESTABLISHMENT IN THE SOUTH

The tale of disestablishment in the South is quickly told. In the early years of the republic the new philosophy of the rights of man was strong south of the Potomac. Leadership was furnished by Virginia, and Virginia had pioneered among the states in the separation of Church and State. Delaware, a northern state which tends to have in it something of the South but even more of Pennsylvania, had required by its constitution of 1776 that all elected to office proclaim themselves under oath to be Trinitarian Christians who believed in the divine inspiration of the Old and New Testaments. Those who voted them into office were subject to no such theological requirements. By 1792 Delaware had a new constitution which provided explicitly for the religious freedom of individuals and groups, and barred any religious test as a qualification for any office or position of public trust. In this it went even beyond its large and powerful neighbor.

North Carolina had always been one of the less tenaciously held outposts of Anglicanism. Its constitution of 1776 barred clergymen from office, limited office to Protestants, and forbade the establishment of any church. The first elimination of these religious provisos came in 1835 when Article XXXII of the North Carolina constitution was amended to permit the election of any Christian to public office. The limitation of non-Christian officeholders disappeared in 1868, when the amended constitution disqualified "all persons who shall deny the being of Almighty God. . . ." One interesting illusion of a step backward was taken in 1835 when the limitation of public office to Protestants was removed: Article XXXIV which forbade the establishment of any church was dropped. The need for forbidding what had become obviously impossible seemed no longer to exist.

South Carolina also adopted a constitution in 1776, an incomplete affair which contained no bill of rights and made no reference to religious freedom. This omission was more than atoned for in 1778, when a revised constitution established the Protestant religion without reference to denomination, restricted membership in the legislature to Protestants, and in Article XXVIII presented a uniquely detailed set of provisions to insure the preservation of a Protestant state. The Protestant state did not long endure. In 1790 the entire concept was discarded, and the lead of Virginia was followed, with a provision for full religious freedom and the enfranchisement of Catholics and other non-Protestants.

The early tale of Georgia is even more quickly told. The constitution of 1777 provided religious freedom, barred a religious test for voters, but limited membership in the legislature to Protestants. This religious test for solons was removed in the constitution of 1789.

Thus ends the story of disestablishment among the original states of the Union. The story does not concern the states later admitted, with a brief exception for Vermont, because a religious establishment never existed in any of them except for the late and highly specialized case of Utah. As always, the case of Rhode Island was unique; no extension of full religious freedom had to be made there because it existed from the start. Elsewhere in New England the fight for disestablishment was long and bitter, and the ground contested inch by inch. To this very day there remains in New Hampshire a few inches of unconquered ground, having a significance only historical—but, in New Hampshire the historical has been the very recent. Those last few inches were successfully defended as recently as 1922 by those who held to old ideas and what once were deemed ideals. Virginia was the true and glorious battlefield where the full rights of man were contested and won by that generation of philosophers and statesmen with which the Old Dominion was blessed in the hour of its birth as an American state. Where Virginia led, the rest of the South followed with reasonable celerity. In the middle states the soil was well prepared for full religious rights in the years before the Revolution. Diversity in New York and an enlightened harmony in Pennsylvania reached the same conclusion quickly, though the roads were very different. In New Jersey and Maryland the battle took longer to win, but victory was complete in the former by 1844 and in the latter by 1826.

Viewing the country as a whole about the year 1845, one might imagine that the issue was closed, that the problem of the relationship between Church and State was solved where the United States was concerned. But the problem of

God and Caesar, like all fundamental problems, is never entirely solved. Phases are solved, whereupon new and un-suspected phases appear. Even as one phase of the Church and State problem ended, a new and difficult phase waited in the off stage of the future. That second phase is not yet entirely a matter of history.

12

The Fourteenth Amendment

The relationship between Church and State in America has had two basic phases. Our consideration of the first phase has been completed. It concerned the relationship between the State and the Protestant churches. That relationship developed with a uniformity which suggests the existence of a social law approaching in validity a natural law. Granted sufficient numerical preponderance, the leading church in an American colony became the established church. The Calvinists were without serious challenge in New England; the Congregational Church was established in New England. The Anglicans were without serious challenge in the colonial South; the Episcopal Church was established in the South. But granted that sufficient numerical preponderance was lost or did not exist, the leading church of an American colony either lost or never acquired the position of establishment. The Dutch of New York were speedily challenged in numbers by the English settlers, and so the Dutch establishment was short-lived. The Catholics of Maryland never were in a majority, and so their colony was a place of refuge where toleration reigned and not a fortress where their church might be established. Only in Rhode Island, where the principle of toleration was stoutly maintained in an age that deemed it anti-Christian, and in Pennsylvania where the principle of the separation of Church and State was adhered to from the start, was the absence of a religious establishment based on principle and not on expediency.

Thus the social law that produced a religious establishment worked quite as well in reverse. The Dutch establishment in New York was the weakest, and it was the first to go. The Anglican establishment in the South was never so strong as the Calvinist establishment in New England, and so its days were more briefly numbered. The Anglican establishment in Virginia yielded to pressure from the Presbyterians and Baptists, and its passing was made a virtue by the philosophy of Madison and Jefferson. The same pressure, reinforced by the conditions of frontier living, ended the Anglican establishment in the Carolinas and Georgia. In New England, where the establishment was strongest, it had the longest life and it took on a new latter-day aspect in the not always tacit alliance between the Congregational Church and the Federalist Party. On the other hand, the conditions which made establishment possible never existed in the states admitted to the Union after Vermont, nor in the territories with the exception of unique Utah. As for the First Amendment to the Constitution of the United States, to the generation for which it was originally written it meant precisely what it said. By the social law referred to, Congress could in practice make no religious establishment for the entire country even if it had been so minded. The philosophy of Madison and Jefferson made acceptance of this fact a virtue.

The second stage of this first phase was reached during the period after the Revolution. To generalize at the expense of some accuracy, one might term the second phase the establishment of Protestantism. This stage was short-lived. Working against it was the liberalism of the eighteenth century, embodied in the philosophy of Madison and Jefferson and rendered effective by the action of the Republican Party. State after state revised its constitution, all in the direction of religious liberalism. In this process no definite pattern is discernible, although the massive influence of Jefferson in Virginia and the Old Dominion's intellectual leadership in the South extended the Virginia pattern to the rest of the area. But in the North the pattern was confused and confusing. Pennsylvania and Delaware dropped the religious test quickly. The adjacent states of New Jersey and Maryland did so slowly and reluctantly. Vermont acted quickly, but New Hampshire has never completed the process. In general, however, the trend toward a separation of Church and State was steady in the early years of the Republic, and by 1845 it appeared to have been completed. Congregationalists had learned to live on terms of equality with Unitarians and Universalists, Episcopalians had accepted in equal fellowship the Baptists, Methodists, and Presbyterians. Something like a religious spectrum had developed along the Atlantic seaboard, and there were no violent clashes of color in the band which ran from the angry red of New Hampshire Calvinism to the placid violet of Georgia Episcopalianism.

It was, however, a phase that was nearly completed by 1845 and not a process. The second phase has comprised the very gradual and still continuing extension to the states of the prohibition against an establishment of religion contained in the First Amendment. The instrument of extension has been the Fourteenth Amendment.

As we have seen, prior to the ratification of the Fourteenth Amendment an established church was possible in any of the thirteen original states and had existed in most of them. Chief Justice Marshall, speaking of the Bill of Rights in 1833, stated, "These Amendments contain no expression indicating an intention to apply them to the State governments. This Court cannot so apply them" (*Barron* v. *Baltimore*, 7 Peters [U.S.] 243). James Bryce, in his authoritative *The American Commonwealth* (1889), says of the First Amendment that it affects ". . . the National Government only, placing no inhibition on the States, and leaving the whole subject to their uncontrolled discretion, though subject to the general guarantee against oppression."

SOVEREIGNTY OF THE STATES UPHELD

The Supreme Court made an explicit ruling on this point in 1845. Almost twenty years before, the city of New Orleans had adopted an ordinance making it illegal to "convey and expose" any dead person in the parochial Church of St. Louis. The ordinance was designed as a public health measure, but its implications where burial services are concerned are obvious. A person charged with breaking this law brought suit to show that it was unconstitutional, since it affected the free exercise of religion. The Supreme Court ruled that the ordinance was not unconstitutional since the First Amendment did not apply to the states. Justice John Catron stated for the Court, "The Constitution of 1789 makes no provision for protecting the citizens of the respective states in their religious liberties; this is left to the state constitutions and laws; nor is there any inhibition imposed by the Constitution of the United States in this respect on the states" (*Permoli* v. *First Municipality No. 1 of New Orleans*, 3 How. 589. 609).

For over one hundred years the complete sovereignty of the states in matters of religion went completely unchallenged. When that sovereignty came to be challenged, and the challenge did not come until the twentieth century was well advanced, it was challenged on the basis of the Four-

teenth Amendment. Within the lifetime of this generation
the constitutional prohibition of an establishment of religion
has been expanded into a prohibition of the reading of the
Bible and the recitation of the Lord's Prayer in the public
schools of America. Our second task is to explain and analyze this expansion.

The Fourteenth Amendment was ratified in 1868. Its
chief purpose, and in the view of many its only purpose, was
to insure the freedom of the Negroes and to protect their
proper status as citizens of the United States. It is not exces-
sively cynical to say that until recently, it has been used for
just about every other purpose to which it could be twisted.
If ever words and phrases have shown that gaseous quality
to which we referred at the outset, it has been the words and
phrases of the Fourteenth Amendment.

The Amendment reads as follows: "No state shall make
or enforce any law which shall abridge the privileges or immunities of citizens of the United States; nor shall any state
deprive any person of life, liberty or property without due
process of law; nor deny to any person within its jurisdiction
the equal protection of the laws." The fundamental purpose
of the amendment was to extend to the states the limitations
imposed on the federal government by the Bill of Rights; its
immediate and intended beneficiaries were the freedmen of
the former slaveholding states. The historic development of
the amendment has been mainly based on a developing interpretation of its due-process and equal-protection clauses.
This interpretation, in turn, is an outgrowth of the relatively
new, substantive theory of law: the substance of a law must
be reasonable for the law to be constitutional. It is hardly
an exaggeration to say that the fundamental relationship of
the Supreme Court to the United States of America was
changed when that concept came to be accepted by the
Justices of the Court.

How the Amendments Differ

There is a basic difference between the First and Fourteenth amendments where the protection of religious rights is concerned. The First Amendment places an explicit limitation of a specific nature upon the Congress of the United States; the Fourteenth Amendment places a generalized limitation of an undefined nature upon the states of the Union. The limitation imposed by the First Amendment admits of little debate and has occasioned none. Congress has never shown the slightest inclination to establish a religion. The limitation imposed by the Fourteenth Amendment admits of endless debate and has come close to eliciting such. The question of applicability to specific situations depends on how the Supreme Court Justices currently interpret the generalized phrases of an amendment couched in terms that invite dispute. What are the privileges and immunities of citizens? Is one a citizen of the United States or a citizen of a particular state of the Union? What is the meaning of *property*? Does *due process* mean legal process or does it mean reasonable process? What comprises *equal protection*? Is equal protection achieved when the rights of the minority are protected while the will of the majority prevails, or is there equal protection only within that common denominator of action to which there is no minority disagreement? If the latter, how small can a minority be and still evoke the common-denominator principle?

These are not hypothetical questions. All of them have been asked and the answers argued, and nearly a century of interpretation has not brought fully accepted answers. One may believe, as the writer does, that the Fourteenth Amendment clearly prohibits attempts to sanction legally the practices currently called *segregation*. There is historic evidence that the Fourteenth Amendment was passed for precisely that purpose. Hon. John A. Bingham (1815–1900) of Ohio, a member of the House of Representatives and framer of the amendment, so interpreted it: "The purpose of the amendment, in the thought of its framers, was to protect by national law the privileges and immunities of all the citizens of the Republic and the inborn rights of every person within its jurisdiction whenever the same shall be abridged or denied by unconstitutional acts of any State."[1] One may believe this and applaud the purpose and yet hold that the extension of the Fourteenth Amendment to matters of religion was not in the mind of Congress when it passed the amendment. It seems to the writer that the application of the Fourteenth Amendment to the issue of segregation is not a matter of interpretation and that the extension to the issue of religion is, and there the difference lies.

Since the extension of the Fourteenth Amendment to issues of a religious nature depends upon a developing interpretation of the amendment, the obvious next step is to trace the stages of that developing interpretation. Three stages can be distinguished. The first extends from the ratification of the amendment in 1868 through 1896. There is no evidence that during these early years anyone in a responsible judicial position thought of the Fourteenth Amendment as a means of guaranteeing in the states the protection of the religious freedom clause of the Bill of Rights. A minority for which Justice Stephen J. Field was the chief spokesman began to take a broader view of the amendment and particularly of its due-process clause, and in time this minority became a majority. The issue of religious freedom, however, was not pertinent to any case.

The second stage extended from 1897 to 1939. During these four decades the Supreme Court gradually extended the application of the Fourteenth Amendment to various freedom clauses of the Bill of Rights, indicating in various opinions that the guarantee of religious freedom was included in its scope.

The third stage started in 1940 and still continues. In that year the Fourteenth Amendment was specifically used in the Jehovah's Witnesses case to guarantee in the states the religious-freedom clause of the First Amendment. Thus, for the first seventy years of its history the Fourteenth Amendment was not cited, in any case directly concerned with a religious issue, as such a guarantee. Before it was so used, a century and a half separated the viewpoint of the Supreme Court majority and the viewpoint of the Founding Fathers, and nearly three quarters of a century separated the Supreme Court viewpoint from that of the Congress which passed the Fourteenth Amendment and the states which ratified it. A long and intricate process of development must be traced, and the tracing of it leads us far from the area of religious issues.

At the usual risks of over-simplification it may be said that the process of development concerned two very different sets of rights, the rights of the freedmen and the rights of corporations. Thus the Fourteenth Amendment developed in two different directions and on two different bases. The first might be termed the moral development. It concerned the rights of Negroes. The second might be termed the economic development. It concerned the rights of corporations. The two patterns of development have little more in common than their common starting point, the amendment itself.

To refer to the former as a process of development is seriously to distort the meaning of words. It was a process of intended atrophy. The tragic victim of action and reaction in the three decades following the adoption of the Fourteenth Amendment was the Negro in whose interests it was adopted. One by one his intended rights were stripped away, as he fell victim successively to inertia and reaction. In intent the Fourteenth Amendment was founded on spiritual and humane values, as were the other liberating amendments. In practice it was made to serve values that were materialistic and economic.

RIGHTS OF NEGROES AND CORPORATIONS

Between 1876 and 1884 the Supreme Court ruled in eight cases involving the rights of Negroes. In 1876 it held unconstitutional the provisions of the Civil Rights Enforcement Act of 1870 which penalized inspectors in state elections for refusing to receive and count votes and for obstructing any citizen from voting (*United States* v. *Reese*, 92 U.S. 214). That took care of the Negro vote. The same year it held that the rights of peaceable assembly and petition for redress of grievances, the right to bear arms and the right to vote were not rights enjoyed under the Constitution, and the Fourteenth Amendment added nothing to rights already possessed. The right to vote, it was held in this decision, came from the states only (*United States* v. *Cruikshank*, 92 U.S. 542). That decision added a few more planks to the coffin in which the rights of Negroes would be buried.

In 1883 the Court held unconstitutional the provision of the Ku Klux Klan Act of 1871 which made it criminal for two or more persons to conspire against the equal protection of the laws and against the privileges and immunities of the laws as applied to others. The Court ruled that the three liberation amendments did not authorize Congress to legislate directly as to the acts of private persons (*United States* v. *Harris*, 106 U.S. 629). The same year the Court held unconstitutional the Civil Rights Act of 1875 which made it a crime for any person to deny to others full and equal enjoyment of the accommodations of inns, public conveyances, and places of amusement. The Court held in the opinion delivered by Justice Bradley that the Fourteenth Amendment did not invest Congress with the power to legislate on subjects within the domain of State legislation, or to create a code of municipal law for the regulation of private rights.

The best treatment of the interpretation of the Fourteenth Amendment is to be found in the definitive study of the Supreme Court published in three volumes in 1923 by Charles Warren, *The Supreme Court in United States History*. Warren concludes that of the enforcement laws only a small part remained even nominally in force. Of the forty-seven sections of the three statutes, forty-two were either repealed, rendered obsolete, or declared invalid by the Court. In the two decades following the passage of the Fourteenth Amendment a series of Supreme Court decisions adverse to the full exercise of civil rights by Negroes largely canceled out the literal and obvious purpose of the liberation amendments. Then were cultivated those grapes of wrath whose bitter wine the mid-twentieth century must drink.

The corporations fared very much better during these decades than did the Negroes, as a series of Supreme Court decisions limited the regulatory powers of the states over corporations and gave the latter the sort of protection accorded by the Bill of Rights to persons. The process started in an abattoir in New Orleans.

On June 1, 1870, there became effective an act of the Louisiana legislature entitled "An act to protect the health of the city of New Orleans, to locate the stock-landings and slaughter-houses and to incorporate 'The Crescent City Live-Stock Landing and Slaughter-House Company.'" The act both created the corporation and vested the seventeen incorporators and their successors with certain special and exclusive privileges, certainly to their benefit and not impossibly to the benefit of certain carpetbag legislators. Meat animals could not be kept or slaughtered in New Orleans or the parishes of Orleans, Jefferson, or St. Bernard except as the act provided. The company was authorized to establish

an abattoir and slaughterhouse on the river below the occu-
pied parts of the city and, it was understandably hoped, out
of olfactory range. Fees for the slaughtering of animals were
to be paid to the company, which had the authority to supervise slaughtering procedures. These exclusive privileges were
to extend for twenty-five years. Since a quarter of a million
people lived in the thousand square miles covered by the
act, the value of the monopoly was substantial. More than
a thousand people previously engaged in the area in the pro-
curing and preparation of meat for the New Orleans mar-
ket were required, as the price of staying in business, to accept the supervision of the corporation and to pay its fees.
An association of butchers brought suit to prevent the law
from going into effect, and the attorney-general of Louisiana
and the corporation brought separate suits to defend it. The
Supreme Court of Louisiana found the act constitutional,
and the plaintiffs carried the case to the Supreme Court of
the United States.

The plaintiffs based their case on the Thirteenth and Fourteenth amendments, particularly on the clause in the latter
which declares that "no State shall make or enforce any law
which shall abridge the privileges or immunities of citizens
of the United States." The Supreme Court, by a five-to-four
vote, upheld the Louisiana court, ruling that the Louisiana
legislature had acted within its prerogatives in creating the
corporation and that the Fourteenth Amendment prohibited
only an invasion of the rights of citizens of the United States
as distinguished from those of citizens of a state. The majority opinion held that the purpose of the liberation amendments was to give freedom to the Negro slaves and to protect them from the oppression of their former masters. It
further held that the Fourteenth Amendment established a
distinction between citizenship of the United States and
citizenship of the several states. It held that the "privileges
and immunities" guaranteed embraced the rights which are

fundamental to citizens under all free governments, denying that it was the purpose of the Fourteenth Amendment to vest the protection of civil rights in the federal government. It then spelled out the privileges and immunities of citizens of the United States which, in its view, are protected by the Fourteenth Amendment. They were the right of the citizen to come to the seat of government, to assert any claim he may have on that government, to transact any business he may have with it, to seek its protection, to share its offices, to engage in administering its functions, to have free access to its seaports, to demand the care and protection of that government over his life, liberty, and property on the high seas or within the jurisdiction of a foreign government, the right peaceably to assemble and petition for redress of grievances, the right to use the navigable waters of the United States, and other similar rights. One notes that in this first attempt to define the rights protected by the Fourteenth Amendment no right of a religious or educational nature is included in the list.

In brief, the majority opinion took a limited view of the purpose of the Thirteenth, Fourteenth, and Fifteenth amendments: they were passed to free the Negro slaves and to preserve their freedom. It drew a distinction between citizenship of the United States and citizenship of a particular state. It maintained that the purpose of the Fourteenth Amendment was to preserve for all American citizens certain enumerated rights that free men habitually have in free societies. It denied that the amendment was designed to protect the citizen of a state against the legislative power of his own state. Implicit in all this is the doctrine enunciated in *McCulloch* v. *Maryland* (1819), that the wisdom of any legislative act is a question for the legislature's judgment. This decision, which had been reinforced by subsequent decisions, meant that a legislature has the right to choose its means to achieve a constitutionally allowable result. The effect of *Mc-*

Culloch v. *Maryland* was to leave the substance of constitutional freedom in the hands of the popularly elected branch of the government.

The minority opinion was written by Justice Field. It neither added to the list of rights enumerated in the majority opinion nor modified it. The minority simply stated, "The amendment does not attempt to confer any new privileges or immunities upon citizens, or to enumerate those already existing. It assumes that there are such privileges and immunities which belong of right to citizens as such, and ordains that they shall not be abridged by state legislation."

Justice Field opened the minority opinion by a consideration of the purpose and meaning of the Thirteenth Amendment, which prohibits slavery and involuntary servitude except for crime. His conclusion was that to be allowed to pursue only one trade or calling and in only one location might not be slavery but was something closely resembling it. The implication was that to be required to pursue the butcher's trade in one specific area of New Orleans bore an analogy to serfdom. He then proceeded to consider the meaning of the Fourteenth Amendment where citizenship was concerned. He denied the concept, which had been upheld by Calhoun and others, that citizenship of the United States derived from citizenship in a particular State. He maintained that the first clause of the Fourteenth Amendment recognized in explicit terms citizenship of the United States ("No State shall make or enforce any law which shall abridge the privileges or immunities of citizens of the United States"), and that after the passage of the amendment a citizen of a state became a citizen of the United States residing in that state. He pointed out that the exercise of these rights and privileges was affected by the condition and local institutions of the state, city, or town where he resided, "but in no other way can they be affected by the action of the State, or by the residence of the citizen therein. They do not derive their existence from its legislation, and cannot be destroyed by its power." Thus Justice Field argued steadily for the freedom of individual action, denied that there is a state citizenship separate from American citizenship, and maintained that personal rights do not derive from state or local legislation and cannot be destroyed by its power.

In the logic of legal interpretation Justice Field's viewpoint was the liberal one and the one that might well have restored to the liberation amendments those spiritual and humane values which they were intended to possess. But in the facts of history the record is otherwise. The minority opinion in the Slaughterhouse Cases fascinated those who were not at all interested in the liberation of the Negro but very much interested in the liberation of the corporation. The minority opinion of Justice Field, in whose own thinking there is a curious ambivalence between humane and economic motivation, seemed to provide a promising means to that end.

In 1876 the Supreme Court heard the case of *Munn* v. *Illinois* (94 U.S. 113), which involved the validity of a law setting rates for grain elevators in the Chicago area. Justice Field, still in the minority, held that the law was unconstitutional under the Fourteenth Amendment. To him the word *liberty* in the Fourteenth Amendment meant "freedom to go where one may choose, and to act in such manner, not inconsistent with the equal rights of others, as his judgment may dictate for the promotion of his happiness; that is, to pursue such callings and avocations as may be most suitable to develop his capacities, and give to them their highest enjoyment." As always, he expounded his argument for economic freedom in language that is moralistic and humane. Chief Justice Waite delivered the majority opinion, holding that the elevators were subject to rate regulation. The significant fact, however, is not that the majority recognized the power of the legislature to set rates. It is the contention that the legislature could regulate the industry because changing conditions had "affected it with a public interest." Presumably if conditions had not changed—whatever that enigmatic phrase may connote—the legislature would not have had the power to set rates. The suggestion is that there is some sort of constitutional limitation on the regulatory power. No such concession had been made by the majority in the Slaughterhouse Cases, in which the decision was based squarely on the thinking of *McCulloch* v. *Maryland*.

"PUBLIC INTEREST"

There is a Janus-like quality to the majority opinion in *Munn* v. *Illinois*. It looked to the past in accepting as valid the principle that the legislature is judge of the wisdom of its own acts. But it looked to the future in its suggestion that the Constitution does set some sort of limitation on state laws affecting economic freedom. It raised a host of undetermined possibilities with its suggestion that "public interest" determines when that limitation is effective and when it is not. Something amorphous called "public interest" had replaced the sovereignty of the legislature as at least a potential norm for court action. Businessmen with an ear to the ground might have murmured, "For protection against the legislature, the corporation can resort to the courts."

They proceeded to resort to the courts, to test the possibilities of this new structure of law which was beginning to rise upon the Fourteenth Amendment. In 1886 the Court decided, in *Santa Clara County* v. *Southern Pacific Railroad* (118 U.S. 394, 396) that a corporation was a "person" within the meaning of the amendment. Let one premise be the thinking of Justice Field and those who agreed with him about the paramount importance of personal liberty. Let the other premise be an interpretation of the Fourteenth

Amendment whereby a corporation is legally a person. Let that thinking and that interpretation be fused in one conclusion, and American industry would have a Magna Charta of inestimable value. Magna Charta was in the process of being written.

In 1887 the next logical step was taken by a Court in which the new economic liberalism now commanded a majority. In *Mugler* v. *Kansas* (123 U.S. 623) the Court knocked the props from under *McCulloch* v. *Maryland,* which had laid the foundation for the long respected doctrine that legislatures should determine the wisdom of regulatory acts. In 1890 this was confirmed in *Chicago, Milwaukee and St. Paul Railroad* v. *Minnesota* (123 U.S. 418). In 1905 the new structure was completed in *Lochner* v. *New York* (198 U.S. 45). A New York law limited work in the baking industry to ten hours a day. The Court held that the law violated freedom of contract. The majority opinion delivered by Justice Peckham held that while such a limitation of working hours might be reasonable when required for reasons of public health, each case had to be decided on the question of whether public health was actually involved. The Court decided that the quality of the bread was not affected by the number of hours a day the bakers worked. Hence the public health was not affected, the general welfare of the people was not at stake, and the New York law was unconstitutional. *Lochner* v. *New York* sounded, as it then seemed, the final death knell of *McCulloch* v. *Maryland.* The entire concept of legislative wisdom went into limbo, not to be resurrected in matters economic until well into the twentieth century.

Warren's investigations revealed some 790 cases between 1889 and 1918 in which statutes were attacked under the due-process and the equal-protection-of-the-law clauses of the Fourteenth Amendment. Of these the great majority arose from issues involving the use of police power. Of the fifty-three cases, however, in which the Court held the statute unconstitutional, two thirds involved the rates and regulation of public service corporations. Only fourteen involved the general rights and liberties of individuals, and only two of these fourteen cases involving what might be termed "social justice legislation" aroused widespread criticism. One was the case involving the work day of the New York bakers, and the other (*Coppage* v. *Kansas*, 236 U.S. 1) held invalid a law forbidding employers to coerce employees not to join a labor union or to remain in one.

Thus, in the decades following its adoption, two distinct and totally divergent trends are to be observed in the interpretation of the Fourteenth Amendment. One trend was to deny to Negroes the full measure of those civil rights it and the other liberating amendments had been adopted to insure in the first instance. The other was to extend to corporations by a series of ever widening interpretations of the amendment a measure of freedom from state regulation that accorded with the spirit of the times but hardly with the spirit of the men who framed the amendments and the American people who adopted them. Thirty years after its passage the Fourteenth Amendment, which was intended to be the charter of Negro freedom, had become the Magna Charta of corporation freedom. Not merely was any application of it to the religious phrases of the First Amendment beyond man's remotest dream; its application to its real purpose, the achievement of legal equality for all Americans, was lulled to a fitful slumber. There is nothing more important in this chapter to the subject of the book than the fact that nothing in the chapter is pertinent to the subject of the book. The nuptials of the First and Fourteenth amendments would not be celebrated for a long, long time to come.

13

Minority Freedom

The first statement by the Supreme Court that may be construed retroactively as an application of the Fourteenth Amendment to the principle contained in the First came in 1871. It came in an opinion signed by only three members of the Court, but it was a majority opinion. Two members were absent, two did not vote, and two dissented. It was the case of *Watson* v. *Jones* (80 U.S. 679, 728).

Watson v. *Jones* was a post-Civil War skirmish fought in a Louisville, Kentucky, church, but one more political than theological. The Presbyterian Church had supported the Emancipation Proclamation and opposed slavery. In May 1865, it adopted resolutions requiring Southerners who wished to be missionaries either to proclaim their disbelief in slavery or to acquire it. The issue came to a head in the Walnut Street Presbyterian Church of Louisville, where a majority of the congregation favored the northern viewpoint as supported by the Presbyterian general assembly, but a southern minority had on its side the trustees, elders, and pastor. An attempt was made by the northern faction, aided by the Presbyterian general assembly and otherwise abetted from the north, to elect officers favorable to the northern viewpoint. The quarrel was brought before a state court which found for the southern side. It was then carried to the United States circuit court of Kentucky and thence to the Supreme Court.

Justice Samuel F. Miller delivered the majority opinion in favor of the northern side, on the grounds that the property in question was not held by an independent congregation but by one subordinate to a general church organization. In the course of his opinion he stated, "The full and free right to entertain any religious belief, to practise any religious principle, and to teach any religious doctrine which does not violate the laws of morality and property, and which does not infringe on personal rights, is conceded to all. The law knows no heresy, and is committed to the support of no dogma, the establishment of no sect." The statement is not explicit, but in its context this is obviously a declaration of religious freedom for minorities. For over seventy years the Fourteenth Amendment would be applied for the protection of minority freedom.

JUSTICE FIELD

In 1879 a federal court gave the first decision applying the Fourteenth Amendment to the protection of religious liberty. It was the work of Justice Field, already mentioned as an apostle of freedom, with emphasis on economic freedom. Stephen J. Field (1816–99) is a fascinating figure in the history of American jurisprudence. One of the nine children of Reverend David Dudley Field, clergyman and antiquarian of Haddam, Connecticut, he came from a family of marked and diversified talents. His older brother David Dudley became a figure to conjure with in American law.

His brother Cyrus promoted the first transatlantic cable. His brother Henry brought to Presbyterian ranks a theological progressivism not entirely acceptable to the entrenched. As a boy Stephen spent two years in the Levant; presumably he is the one Justice in the history of the Supreme Court able to speak Greek. He graduated from Williams College in 1837, after sitting on the other end of the log from Mark Hopkins. From this legendary preceptor he learned his rhetoric, in which he excelled; his logic, at which some have caviled; his natural theology; and his metaphysics. All his life he believed that the facts of life are best evaluated by the application of a few established principles. Some have maintained that he could apply his logic, buttressed by natural theology and metaphysical wit, with the full force of his rhetoric, which inclined to the Old Testament model, in the cause of diametrically opposite principles and do so without a qualm of conscience. And this may be. His convictions were sincere and intense, but that he was fallible was never one of them. Furthermore, who can say that in the farther metaphysical reaches the arguments for the freedom of a corporation may not have a kinship with the arguments for the freedom of a minority religious group? This much is certain: a belief in freedom was one of Field's established principles.

He sailed to San Francisco in 1849, landed with ten dollars in his pocket but spent seven of them to get his trunks ashore. With his three dollars approximately intact he made his way to Maryville, in the gold country, contracted to purchase sixty-five town lots, formed a local government, and got himself elected mayor. It is well for those critical of the conservative mind not to confuse it with the stodgy. Prosperity came quickly, as well it might to such a man, but it was blighted by a feud with a newly appointed state judge which led to Field's being disbarred, reinstated, disbarred again, jailed, fined, and threatened with imminent and complete extinction. Nothing came of the last, but Field, with his inheritance of Connecticut prudence, learned to shoot through his pocket. When things quieted down, he resumed his program of self-betterment, built a lucrative law practice in Maryville, and drafted the civil and criminal practice acts for California. In 1857 he was elected to the state supreme court.

The Supreme Court of the United States needed a member skilled in the land and mining cases coming from the Pacific coast. Field was an obvious expert, and on March 10, 1863, he was appointed to the Supreme Court by President Lincoln. He stayed on the bench until December 1, 1897, exceeding Marshall's incumbency by two months. He was the last Lincoln appointee to leave the bench. During his thirty-four years as a Supreme Court Justice he did more than any other member to mold a pattern of judicial thought based on the guarantees of the Fourteenth Amendment. That pattern was designed to free American business from the trammels of state legislation, but behind it in the mind of Justice Field was one of those few established principles he had learned from Mark Hopkins. Field believed in freedom. That was the glory of Justice Field. The limitation was that he thought of freedom primarily in terms of the corporation.

He could think of it, however, in other terms. In 1879 he delivered an opinion which at least intimated that the Fourteenth Amendment was applicable to the protection of religious liberty. He stated, "In our country hostile and discriminating legislation by a statute against persons of any class, sect, creed or nation, or whatever form it may be expressed is forbidden by the Fourteenth Amendment" (*Ho Ah Kow* v. *Numan*, 12 Fed. Cas. No. 6546, pp. 252, 256). In 1885 he expanded this doctrine: "The Fourteenth Amendment . . . undoubtedly intended not only that there should be no arbitrary deprivation of life or liberty, or arbitrary spoliation of property, but that equal protection and security should be given to all under like circumstances in the enjoyment of their personal and civil rights . . ." (*Barbier* v. *Connolly,* 113 U.S. 27, 31). His point of view was shared in various dissenting opinions by Justice John M. Harlan (1833–1911), but the Supreme Court majority continued to take the limited view that the purpose of the amendment was to protect the rights of the freedmen and continued to disregard its possible applicability to cases involving religion.

Evidence of this limited viewpoint can be found in an opinion delivered by Chief Justice Waite in 1887: "That the first ten Articles of Amendment were not intended to limit the powers of the state governments in respect to their own people, but to operate on the National Government alone, was decided more than a half century ago, and that decision has been steadily adhered to since . . ." (*Spies* v. *Illinois,* 123 U.S. 166). In 1891 a United States circuit court went further: "The fourteenth amendment of the Constitution of the United States has not abrogated the Sunday laws of the States, and established religious freedom therein. The States may establish a Church or Creed, and maintain them, as far as the Federal Constitution is concerned. . . . As a matter of fact they [the Founding Fathers] left the States the most absolute power on the subject, and any of them might, if they chose, establish a creed and a church and maintain them" (*in re King,* 46 F. 905, 912). The Fourteenth Amendment was in force fifty years before the Supreme Court, in a majority opinion, even implied that it guaranteed to the citizens of the individual states the right to religious freedom. It finally did so in 1923, in *Meyer* v. *Nebraska.*

TEACHING GERMAN IN NEBRASKA

In 1919 the Nebraska legislature passed an act forbidding the teaching of any subject in a language other than English and, in an extraordinary venture into the field of pedagogy, forbade the teaching of any foreign language in a Nebraska school below the ninth grade. Behind the act was the emotional ferment that attended World War I. The shadow of the Kaiser still lay across the cornfields; it was alleged that private and parochial schools which taught in German were hotbeds of alien sentiment. Robert T. Meyer, a teacher in a school maintained by the Evangelical Lutheran Congregation, was charged with teaching German through a collection of Bible stories to a child who had not completed the eighth grade. He testified that his "ultimate and only object (was) . . . that the children can take part in the devotional exercises of the parents at home, attend public worship with the parents and worship with them— for that reason we wanted to have children learn so much German that they could worship with their parents."[1] The Nebraska supreme court found that social and national integrity was threatened by this practice and therefore that the challenged act was a reasonable exercise of the police power of the state (*Nebraska District of Evangelical Lutheran Synod of Missouri et al.* v. *McKelvie,* 175 N.W. 531).

The case was brought to the Supreme Court on the grounds that the act deprived Meyer of liberty without due process of law. The majority opinion, to which Justices Holmes and Sutherland dissented, was written by Justice McReynolds. He pointed out that the Court had never attempted to define with exactness the liberty guaranteed by the Fourteenth Amendment. He found that liberty included ". . . the right of the individual to contract, to engage in any of the common occupations of life, to acquire useful knowledge, to marry, establish a home, and bring up children, to worship God according to the dictates of his own conscience and, generally, to enjoy those privileges long recognized at common law as essential to the orderly pursuit of happiness by free men. . . . The established doctrine is that this liberty may not be interfered with, under the guise of protecting the public interest, by legislative action which is arbitrary or without reasonable relation to some purpose within the competency of the state to effect. Determination by the legislature of what constitutes proper exercise of the police power is not final or conclusive, but is subject to supervision by the courts" (*Meyer* v. *State of Nebraska,* 262 U.S. 390). Justice McReynolds concluded that although ". . . the state may do much, go very far, indeed, in order to improve the quality of its citizens physically, mentally, and morally," it could not deprive foreign-language teachers of their calling nor parents of the right to control the education of their children.

It should be noted that the majority opinion gave an oblique rather than a direct guarantee to religious freedom from state action. In the immediate sense the point at issue in *Meyer* v. *Nebraska* was the right of Nebraska parents of foreign extraction to have their children educated in schools conducted in the language of their homeland. In a broader sense but still a direct one, it guaranteed the right of parents to send a child to a private school of their choosing. What was not contested, and indeed could not be in the light of the auspices under which the school was conducted, was the fact that training in this school had religious connotations; indeed, Meyer based his defense upon that fact. In *Meyer* v. *Nebraska* the Supreme Court spelled out the right of educational freedom as one of the rights of Americans protected against state invasion by the due-process clause of the Fourteenth Amendment. On the precedent set in *Meyer* v. *Nebraska* there came two years later a finding, much better known, in what is usually referred to as the Oregon school case.

THE OREGON SCHOOL CASE

Behind the Oregon school case was also an undercurrent of thought, or more accurately of emotion, that was part of the tidal wave of emotion that swept the country during World War I days. To what extent the fervor of devotion for public education then evidenced, especially in states across the broad Mississippi, could be attributed to purely pedagogic motivation is open to question. Analysis would probably reveal more than a trace of religious prejudice in its composition, and probably at least a trace of nativist prejudice. The old idea that the newer races and their churches and institutions posed a threat to Americanism died hard. The initiative and referendum provision of Oregon law gave that sort of thinking a chance to express itself in popular legislative action.

The initiative, if not the referendum, has largely passed into America's legal limbo, but a half century ago many thought that all that was needed to produce Utopia in the Northwest was to give the people the power to make their laws directly. In 1902 Oregon adopted the initiative and referendum. By the former, laws could be enacted by the voters without action by any branch of the state government; by the latter, legislation passed by the state government could be repealed. The signature of 8 per cent of the voters of the state placed any proposal, including a constitutional amendment, on the ballot. The signature of 5 per cent of the voters could force a referendum on any proposition enacted by the legislature. It was democracy, pure, simple—and fallacious.

The voters of Oregon did many things. They abolished the Wallowa County high school, increased the bounty on jack rabbits, forbade the smoking of cigarettes, prohibited compulsory vaccination for smallpox, moved the state university forty-one miles farther north, and buried under an avalanche of votes the building of a power-distribution system from Bonneville Dam which had been wildly hailed as a source of power by the very voters who vetoed the moving of the power. The above is a close paraphrase of the record as reported by a distinguished and rueful Oregonian, Richard L. Neuberger.[2] Neuberger further records the memorable day when the voters, in response to the charge of gill-net fishermen that the operators of fish wheelers were killing salmon fishing in the Columbia River and the countercharge of the latter that the former were doing it, with Draconian severity forbade both kinds of fishing. This effectively killed one of the state's leading industries until the scorned legislature saved the day. His fascinating record of democracy unsullied and direct finally records what was the last logical development prior to the repeal of the initiative. Direct legislation became such a welter of self-seeking that the same Oregonians, who were willing to sign any petition to get rid of the people seeking their signatures, made it an inflexible rule to vote No on all proposals. But the Oregon school law came a bit earlier.

Neuberger tells the story: "In 1922 the State was gripped by Ku Klux Klan hysteria. Fiery crosses burned on the hills, and initiative petitions to close all religious and private schools were circulated in the streets and marketplaces. Sufficient signatures were obtained in a few days. The measure was adopted at the polls, 115,506 votes to 103,685. What no legislature had ever dared to do, the people had done with the weapon of 'the Oregon system.'" Specifically, the Compulsory Education Act, adopted November 7, 1922, required every child between eight and sixteen years to be sent to "a public school for the period of time a public school shall be held during the current year" in the district where the child resided. Failure to do so was declared a misdemeanor, and exceptions were unimportant. The act was to become effective on September 1, 1926.

The case was carried to the Supreme Court by the Sisters of the Holy Name of Jesus and Mary. It was also tested in *Pierce* v. *Hill Military Academy*, but the Supreme Court made its finding in *Pierce* v. *Society of Sisters* (268 U.S. 510) on appeal from the District Court of the United States for the District of Oregon. The point at issue was the constitutional right of a religious organization to operate a religious-oriented, alias parochial, school in the face of a contrary state policy affirmed by the voters. The decision, again delivered by Justice McReynolds, who this time spoke for a unanimous Court, was in the affirmative.

Justice McReynolds pointed out that the Society of Sisters, which had been organized in 1880, had long conducted orphanages, primary schools, high schools, and junior colleges. The inevitable result of enforcing the act, he stated, would be to destroy the primary schools conducted by the Sisters and perhaps all other private, primary schools for normal children in the State of Oregon. "Under the doctrine of *Meyer* v. *Nebraska*, 262 U.S. 390, we think it entirely plain that the Act of 1922 unreasonably interferes with the liberty of parents and guardians to direct the upbringing and education of children under their control. As often heretofore pointed out, rights guaranteed by the Constitution may not be abridged by legislation which has no reasonable relation to some purpose within the competency of the State. The fundamental theory of liberty upon which all governments in this Union repose excludes any general power of the State to standardize its children by forcing them to accept instruction from public teachers only. The child is not the mere creature of the State; those who nurture and direct his destiny have the right, coupled with the high duty, to recognize and prepare him for additional obligations. The decrees below are affirmed" (*Pierce* v. *Society of Sisters*, 268 U.S. 510).

These two cases gave to parochial schools their legal guarantee of existence. The principle was established in the first and applied in the second: churches have the right to conduct schools subject to the reasonable supervisory powers of the state, and parents have the right to send their children to them. In each case the Supreme Court protected a religious minority in the exercise of a right which could hardly be said to have a common border with the corresponding right of the majority. Nebraska Lutherans of German extraction could send their children to private schools in which classes were conducted in German; the majority of Cornhuskers would continue to send their children to public schools, or indeed to private schools, where classes were conducted in English. Oregon Catholics could send their children to parochial schools if they chose; they and all other Oregonians also could send them to public schools. In retrospect, after emotion was happily allayed, the application in these cases of the Fourteenth Amendment to the Bill of Rights was clear and incontestable. Minority religious rights were protected; majority rights were in no sense concerned.

ENTER JEHOVAH'S WITNESSES

For some years there was peace on the Church and State front, and then the peace was disturbed by the Jehovah's Witnesses issue. But before this issue arose, the Court in several cases reaffirmed its stand on the application of the Fourteenth Amendment to personal rights. In 1925, in a case involving a New York statute against "criminal anarchy," the Court ruled that freedom of speech and of the press "are among the fundamental personal rights and 'liberties' protected by the due process clause of the Fourteenth Amendment from impairment by the States" (*Gitlow* v. *New York,* 268 U.S. 652, 666). It was widely inferred that freedom of speech and of the press carried as an inevitable corollary freedom of religion. In 1934 the Court ruled that required military training at a state university did not infringe upon the liberty of a conscientious objector. Justice Cardozo joined Justices Brandeis and Stone in a concurring opinion: "I assume for present purposes that the religious liberty protected by the First Amendment against invasion by the nation is protected by the Fourteenth Amendment against invasion by the states. . . . The First Amendment, if it be read into the Fourteenth, makes invalid any state law 'respecting an establishment of religion or prohibiting the free exercise thereof'" (*Hamilton* v. *University of California,* 293 U.S. 245).

Little by little the Fourteenth Amendment, which as a matter of historic fact had been adopted to secure the legal right of the freedmen and as a matter of another historic fact had been adapted to secure the legal rights of corporations, was being extended to secure the rights of all Americans against state infringement. Charles Warren sums up the history of the decisions about the applicability to state action of the fundamental guarantees of the Bill of Rights in the following words: "Thus, we have this situation: in 1907, the Court expressly left the question undecided; in 1920, it stated that it did not consider it or decide it, but simply conceded it for the purposes of the case; in 1922, it stated that the Federal Constitution 'imposes upon the States no obligation to confer upon those within their jurisdiction either the right of free speech or the right of silence.' Yet, in 1925, it stated that 'we may and do assume' that freedom of speech and of the press is one of the 'fundamental personal rights and liberties' protected by the Due Process Clause. And hence, in 1925, the Court adopted as the law on this point, the dissenting opinions of Judge Harlan in 1907, and of Judge Brandeis in 1920."[3]

An attempt was made in 1937, in a case involving double jeopardy, to extend this applicability all the way. In *Palko* v. *State of Connecticut* (309 U.S. 319, 326) the appellant argued that whatever would be a violation of the Bill of Rights if done by the federal government would be equally illegal if done by the states because of the Fourteenth Amendment. The Court was not ready to go that far. In an opinion in which all concurred except Justice Butler, Justice Cardozo drew a distinction between fundamental liberties and those of secondary importance. Placing freedom of thought and speech among the fundamental freedoms, he stated: "Of that condition one may say that it is the matrix, the indispensable condition, of nearly every other form of freedom. With rare aberrations a pervasive recognition of that truth can be traced in our history, political and legal. So it has come about that the domain of liberty, withdrawn by the Fourteenth Amendment from encroachment by the states, has been enlarged by latter-day judgments to include liberty of the mind as well as liberty of action."

This point would not be clinched, however, until a ruling was made in a case in which the exercise of minority rights and the exercise of majority rights had a clear-cut common border. It finally came in two cases, in 1940 in *Minersville School District* v. *Gobitis* and in 1943 in *West Virginia State Board of Education* v. *Barnette*. Both cases involved Jehovah's Witnesses.

As is so often true in the law, there was skirmishing around the legal outposts before the central conflict was resolved. The first skirmish took place in 1938. A Jehovah's Witness was arrested for distributing without a permit tracts that set forth the gospel of the "Kingdom of Jehovah." Her defense was that she had been sent by Jehovah "to do His Work" and that to apply for a permit for this high purpose would be "an act of disobedience to His Commandment." She was found guilty and, in default of the payment of a fine, was sentenced to fifty days in jail. The case was brought to the Supreme Court which found the ordinance requiring a permit unconstitutional, ruling that "it strikes at the very foundation of the freedom of the press by subjecting it to license and censorship" (*Lovell* v. *City of Griffin,* 303 U.S. 444).

The Witnesses won a second victory over a state in 1940, this time in a case directly involving freedom of religion. A Connecticut statute required approval by a named public official before one could solicit funds for "any alleged religious, charitable, or philanthropic cause." Jehovah's Witnesses were arrested in New Haven for trying to sell their religious literature without such a certificate of authorization. They were convicted by the court of common pleas of New Haven County, and their conviction was sustained by the supreme court of errors of Connecticut. The Supreme Court of the United States unanimously decided that the act in question was unconstitutional since it deprived the appellants of their liberty without due process of law, in violation of the Fourteenth Amendment.

"The fundamental concept of liberty embodied in that Amendment embraces the liberties guaranteed by the First Amendment. The First Amendment declares that Congress shall make no law respecting an establishment of religion or prohibiting the free exercise thereof. The Fourteenth Amendment has rendered the legislatures of the states as incompetent as Congress to enact such laws." The Court held that the state might, by general and non-discriminatory legislation, regulate such solicitation on its streets. It added, however, "The appellants are right in their insistence that the Act in question is not such a regulation. . . . The appellants urge that to require them to obtain a certificate as a condition of soliciting support for their views amounts to a prior restraint on the exercise of their religion within the meaning of the Constitution. . . . Such a censorship of religion as the means of determining its right to survival is a denial of liberty protected by the First Amendment and included in the liberty which is within the protection of the Fourteenth" (*Cantwell et al.* v. *The State of Connecticut,* 310 U.S. 296, 303). This decision, delivered by Justice Owen J. Roberts on May 20, 1940, is the first in which the Court explicitly held that the Fourteenth Amendment is applicable to the religious guarantees of the Bill of Rights.

It should be noted that in neither of these cases did the exercise of minority rights and the exercise of majority rights have a clear-cut common border. In both cases the Court found, in the spirit of John Milton's *Areopagitica,* that to license the press strikes at the very heart of its freedom. But in both situations, involving as they did the distribution of religious literature, the right of the majority to ignore such literature remained crystal-clear and fully effective. It was a right fully exercised by the great majority of Americans, who went their ways seeking the message of Jehovah or ignoring it according to the dictates of their consciences. Again minority rights were protected, but majority rights were in no sense concerned.

THE FLAG SALUTE

Then came the two flag-salute cases. To quote from the Supreme Court opinion in the second (*West Virginia State Board of Education* v. *Barnette,* 319 U.S. 624), "The Witnesses are an unincorporated body teaching that the obligation imposed by law of God is superior to that of laws enacted by temporal government. Their religious beliefs include a literal version of Exodus, Chapter 20, verses 4 and 5, which says: 'Thou shalt not make unto thee any graven image, or any likeness of anything that is in heaven above, or that is in the earth beneath, or that is in the water under the earth; thou shalt not bow down thyself to them nor serve them.' They consider that the flag is an 'image' within this command. For this reason they refuse to salute it."

The requirement that schools open the day with a salute to the flag is a commonplace in American education. When youthful Witnesses refused to salute, they were expelled from schools. Their parents were prosecuted, and the reformatory under the various euphemistic aliases it bears in this age of juvenile delinquents loomed before them. State court after court found against the Witnesses. Then, with a curious reversal of the habitual process, the Gobitis case reached the Supreme Court. A Pennsylvania court found that a school regulation requiring the salute to the flag despite sincere religious convictions to the contrary was a violation of the Constitution. The school board carried the case to the Supreme Court. The Court found, in *Minersville School District* v. *Gobitis* (310 U.S. 586) that the promotion of national cohesion through the compulsory flag salute was an interest more important than the preservation of religious freedom. It assumed the power of the state to require the flag salute. Granted the assumption, the finding in the Gobitis case was inevitable. The Pennsylvania court was reversed and the state statute sustained. The year was 1940, war was imminent, the atmosphere was that of wartime, and emotions ran high even beneath judicial robes. Only Justice Stone stood out against the opinion. Yet three years later, the Court reversed itself in the most startling judicial reversal in American history. In 1943 a five to three decision in *West Virginia State Board of Education* v. *Barnette* threw out the Gobitis finding and stated that the required flag salute was a violation of the First and Fourteenth amendments in the case of students with a conscientious objection to it grounded upon religious belief. To this day the Barnette decision remains our high-water mark in the protection of genuine minority religious rights.

The majority opinion was written by Justice Jackson with great care and at substantial length. He opened, as was inevitable, by a description of the finding in the Gobitis case. He gave the description of the Jehovah's Witnesses already quoted. Then he passed to a recognition of the fact that there might be something in this case absent from other cases involving the religious rights of minorities, and proceeded to deny its existence. "The freedom asserted by these appellees does not bring them into collision with rights asserted by any other individual. It is such conflicts which most frequently require intervention of the State to determine where the rights of one end and those of another begin. But the refusal of these persons to participate in the ceremony does not interfere with or deny rights of others to do so. Nor is there any question in this case that their behavior is peaceable and orderly. The sole conflict is between authority and rights of the individual." In short, he recognized that a conflict between the rights of a majority willing to salute the flag and a minority unwilling to do so could theoretically exist. This is the point of departure from the reasoning behind the Gobitis verdict. In the latter, the existence of such a conflict and the implications that it carried lay at the heart of the finding.

There followed a discussion of symbolism and its significance, and then came a telling point: "To sustain the compulsory flag salute we are required to say that a Bill of Rights which guards the individual's right to speak his own mind, left it open to public authorities to compel him to utter what is not in his mind." The basic question, then, is the power of government under the Constitution to enforce acceptance of a patriotic creed; if that power exists, the grounds on which it is exercised cannot be decided by the courts. "Hence validity of the asserted power to force an American citizen publicly to profess any statement of belief or to engage in any ceremony of assent to one, presents questions of power that must be considered independently of any idea we may have as to the utility of the ceremony in question."

Justice Jackson then questioned the axiom on which the Gobitis decision was based, that the state did have the power to impose the discipline of a salute to the flag upon school children. He maintained that nothing basic was involved when one questioned the axiom, doubting that ". . . the strength of government to maintain itself would be impressively vindicated by our confirming power of the State to expel a handful of children from school. . . . Government of limited power need not be anemic government." His next point was quickly established: despite the substantial powers of boards of education, they also are subject to constitutional limitations.

Then comes a passage in his opinion which we can confidently feel reflects some heated closed-chamber debate. Justice Frankfurter, in his dissenting opinion, held in effect that the place for the Jehovah's Witnesses to seek exemption from the compulsory flag salute was the legislative hall and not the courtroom. Such had been the viewpoint of the Court in the Gobitis case, in which it was held proper to "fight out the wise use of legislative authority in the form of public opinion and before legislative assemblies rather than to transfer such a contest to the judicial arena." Following but not citing the viewpoint expressed by Justice Cardozo in *Palko* v. *State of Connecticut*, Justice Jackson said, "The very purpose of a Bill of Rights was to withdraw certain subjects from the vicissitudes of political controversy, to place them beyond the reach of majorities and officials and to establish them as legal principles to be applied by the courts. One's right to life, liberty, and property, to free speech, a free press, freedom of worship and assembly, and other fundamental rights may not be submitted to vote; they depend on the outcome of no elections." Down the halls of time drifts the echo: "inalienable rights." Still basing his argument on Justice Cardozo's distinction between fundamental rights and those of secondary importance, he continued, "The test of legislation which collides with the Fourteenth Amendment, because it also collides with the principles of the First, is much more definite than the test when only the Fourteenth is involved. Much of the vagueness of the due process clause disappears when the specific prohibitions of the First become its standard. The right of a State to regulate, for example, a public utility may well include, so far as the due process test is concerned, power to impose all of the restrictions which a legislature may have a 'rational basis' for adopting. But freedoms of speech and of press, of assembly, and of worship may not be infringed on such slender grounds. They are susceptible of restriction only to prevent grave and immediate danger to interests which the State may lawfully protect. It is important to note that while it is the Fourteenth Amendment which bears directly upon the State, it is the more specific limiting principles of the First Amendment that finally govern this case."

Finally he reached the heart of the Gobitis opinion, that "National unity is the basis of national security" and therefore that authorities have "the right to select appropriate means for its attainment." This case did not involve a national unity to be achieved by persuasion and example. "The problem is whether under our Constitution compulsion as here employed is a permissible means for its achievement." Considering the historical failure of coerced unanimity, he concluded, "Compulsory unification of opinion achieves only the unanimity of the graveyard. . . . If there is any fixed star in our constitutional constellation, it is that no official, high or petty, can prescribe what shall be orthodox in politics, nationalism, religion, or other matters of opinion or force citizens to confess by word or act their faith therein."

In the Barnette case at last we have a situation in which the presumptive right of the majority and the presumptive right of the minority have a clear-cut common border. The presumptive right of the majority is to achieve national security through national unity by means appropriate to its attainment. A means appropriate and effective is the cultivation of patriotism. The salute to the flag is a piece of symbolism which, like all symbolism, may become trite through long repetition. But it may also become ingrained through long repetition. Generation after generation of American school children have started their school days by saluting the flag. The salute to the flag has been part of the framework of their daily lives, a daily act of faith in the principles of their nation and their society, a daily profession of loyalty to that nation and society. We may not say with certainty that in the fetid jungles of Guadalcanal, on the blazing beachhead of Normandy, in the fog-swathed north Atlantic and the blackness of the night sky over Germany men strengthened themselves by murmuring, "I pledge allegiance to the Flag. . . ." Yet the thought, however inchoate, was in their minds and hearts. It is significant that the one war picture which has endured portrays the raising of the flag on a distant Pacific island. The majority of Americans believe in the flag salute, not as an empty piece of symbolism but as an act that strengthens the will, elicits the inner nobility, fosters the spirit of sacrifice in the common cause. The majority has the right to do so.

But, as Justice Frankfurter said in a dissenting opinion that never really came to grips with the philosophic foundation of the majority opinion, "patriotism cannot be enforced by the flag salute." To the Jehovah's Witnesses it is an act forbidden by Holy Writ. To create an intolerable conflict in the human mind between what it deems the ordainments of the Almighty and the ordainments of society strengthens loyalty to neither. The Court with wisdom and in its best tradition recognized that this conflict existed in the minds of the Jehovah's Witnesses. It recognized that it is both unconstitutional and unwise to try to force men's minds. In practice, the young Jehovah's Witnesses could abstain from the flag salute without impairing the right of the majority to perform the salute. No one on either side ever suggested that because the flag salute was contrary to the religious convictions of a minority it should be declared unconstitutional. The salute to the flag fared better than the Lord's Prayer. It fared better because in 1943 the Court acted on the conviction that minority rights should be protected, but not at the expense of majority rights. And so the salute to the flag continues to be part of the framework of the daily lives of American school children, a daily act of faith in the principles of their nation and their society, a daily profession of loyalty to them both.

TEXTBOOKS IN NEW JERSEY

To pass from patriotism to pocketbook is an exercise in bathos, but the record now calls for such a passage. Certain cases, not nearly so frequent in Supreme Court history as in the history of the state courts, combine governmental principle and financial interest in a way not always simple to separate. Such cases depend upon the claim that the taxpayer's property is taken without due process of law. Such a claim underlay the case of *Cochran* v. *Louisiana State Board of Education,* on which a ruling was made in 1930, and in *Everson* v. *Board of Education,* which was settled in 1947. The cases had similar points at issue and were settled in the same way, but the old and the new in Supreme Court thinking are well illustrated in two findings that are fundamentally identical in conclusion but profoundly different in premises.

Two acts of the Louisiana legislature passed in 1928 provided that schoolbooks be loaned without charge to school children of the state. The law drew no distinction between children attending public schools and those attending private schools, inside and outside church auspices. The appellants brought a taxpayers' suit claiming a violation of the Fourteenth Amendment. Both the trial court and the state supreme court refused to issue an injunction against the distribution of textbooks to children attending non-public schools. The Supreme Court of the United States upheld the state courts, citing the opinion of the state supreme court as the foundation of its own opinion: "One may scan the acts in vain to ascertain where any money is appropriated for the purchase of schoolbooks for the use of any church, private sectarian, or even public school. The appropriations were made for the specific purpose of purchasing schoolbooks for the use of the school children of the state, free of cost to them. It was for their benefit and the resulting benefit to the state that the appropriations were made. True, those children attend some school, public or private, the latter sectarian or nonsectarian, and that the books are to be furnished them for their use, free of cost, whichever they attend. The schools, however, are not the beneficiaries of these appropriations. . . . The school children and the state alone are the beneficiaries. It is also true that the sectarian schools, which some of the children attend, instruct their children in religion, and books are used for that purpose, but one may search diligently the acts, though without result, in an effort to find anything to the effect that it is the purpose of the state to furnish religious books for the use of such children. . . . What the statutes contemplate is that the same books that are furnished children attending public schools shall be furnished children attending private schools. This is the only practical way of interpreting and executing the statutes, and this is what the state board of education is doing. Among these books, naturally, none is to be expected adapted to religious instruction."

The conclusion of the Supreme Court followed logically from these factual premises: "Viewing the statute as having the effect thus attributed to it, we cannot doubt that the taxing power of the state is exerted for a public purpose. The legislation does not segregate private schools, or their pupils, as its beneficiaries or attempt to interfere with any matters of exclusively private concern. Its interest is education, broadly; its method, comprehensive. Individual interests are aided only as the common interest is safeguarded" (*Cochran* v. *Louisiana State Board of Education*, 281 U.S. 370).

The viewpoint of the Court in 1930 is crystal-clear. It drew a distinction among the People, the State, and the Church. It held that there was no violation of the Fourteenth Amendment in a specific legislative act designed to benefit the people and the State. Some of the people were being educated in schools operated by a church. The fact of education benefits the people and the State; that it may also benefit the Church is a correlative fact but not an indistinguishable one. So long as the textbooks lent were the same ones lent in the public schools and so long as they were lent for the same purpose, education in the areas of secular study, the act was a piece of social legislation within the constitutional prerogative of the State. Such was the unanimous opinion of the Supreme Court as delivered by Chief Justice Hughes.

THE SCHOOL BUS CASE

Seventeen years later the Court delivered a majority opinion, with four Justices dissenting, in what has come to be known as the New Jersey bus case. In *Everson* v. *Board of Education* (330 U.S. 1) both Justice Black, who delivered the majority opinion, and Justice Jackson, who spoke for the minority, gave lengthy opinions buttressed by appeals to history. The specific point at issue was a New Jersey statute authorizing school districts to make rules and contracts for the transportation of children to and from schools. The Board of Education of Ewing Township authorized reimbursement to parents of bus fares paid by their children en route to school on the regular buses operated by the local transportation system. Some of these children attended Catholic parochial schools. An unusual quirk in the case was provided by the fact that the children used the regular bus service along with the general traveling public. Parochial school children were not being transported in school buses of the ordinary sort.

A taxpayer of the township brought suit on the grounds that the statute violated both the state and federal constitutions. He was sustained by a state court, but the New Jersey Court of Errors and Appeals reversed the finding, and the case was brought to the Supreme Court. In the majority opinion Justice Black first considered the contention that by authorizing the state to take by taxation the private property of some and bestow it on others, the statute violated the due-process clause of the Fourteenth Amendment. Following the reasoning accepted as valid by the entire Court in the Louisiana textbook case, he argued: "Nor does it follow that a law has a private rather than a public purpose because it provided that tax-raised funds will be paid to reimburse individuals on account of money spent by them in a way which furthers a public program. . . . Subsidies and loans to individuals such as farmers and home-owners, and to privately owned transportation systems, as well as many other kinds of businesses, have been commonplace practices in our state and national history." The argument rested squarely on the constitutional right of a state to legislate for a public need. "The fact that a state law, passed to satisfy a public need, coincides with the personal desires of the individuals most directly affected is certainly an inadequate reason for us to say that a legislature has erroneously appraised the public need. . . . Changing local conditions create new local problems which may lead a state's people and its local authorities to believe that laws authorizing new types of public services are necessary to promote the general well-being of the people. The Fourteenth Amendment did not strip the states of their power to meet problems previously left for individual solution. . . ."

Justice Black then turned his attention to a very different matter: "Insofar as the second phase of the due process argument may differ from the first, it is by suggesting that taxation for transportation of children to church schools constitutes support of a religion by the State. But if the law is invalid for this reason, it is because it violates the First Amendment's prohibition against the establishment of religion by law."

At this point the new thinking reveals itself, even when refutation is the final outcome. In the Louisiana textbook case the issue was settled when it was determined that to lend textbooks for the study of secular subjects by private and parochial school children served a legally valid social purpose. In the New Jersey bus case the issue was not settled, even in the mind of the majority who viewed equally secular bus rides by parochial children as serving a social purpose.

Justice Black proceeded to write an outline of the history of religious intolerance in Europe and America, and the long, hard struggle for religious tolerance and freedom. He lauded the contributions of Jefferson and Madison to the latter ideals. He stated, "The 'establishment of religion' clause of the First Amendment meant at least this: Neither a state nor the Federal Government can set up a church. Neither can pass laws which aid one religion, aid all religions, or prefer one religion over another. . . . No tax in any amount, large or small, can be levied to support any religious activities or institutions, whatever they may be called, or whatever form they may adopt to teach or practice religion." And then he came down to the final question. Is a free bus ride for a parochial school child a tax levied to support a religious activity or institution? A question that the Supreme Court did not even bother to ask in 1930, since the textbooks involved were secular, was gravely asked in 1947 by both sides of a divided Court, and given different answers.

Justice Black maintained that the New Jersey statute must be considered in the light of the limitations of the First Amendment. He revealed at least a deference to minority opinion, if not a measure of distrust in his own, when he added, "But we must not strike that state statute down if it is within the State's constitutional power even though it approaches the verge of that power." He held it obvious that New Jersey could not contribute tax funds to the support of any institution that taught the tenets of any church. "On the other hand, other language of the amendment commands that New Jersey cannot hamper its citizens in the free exercise of their own religion. Consequently, it cannot exclude individual Catholics, Lutherans, Mohammedans, Baptists, Jews, Methodists, Non-believers, Presbyterians, or the members of any other faith, *because of their faith, or lack of it* (italics in the original), from receiving the benefits of public welfare legislation. While we do not mean to intimate that a state could not provide transportation only to children attending public schools, we must be careful, in protecting the citizens of New Jersey against state-established churches, to be sure that we do not inadvertently prohibit New Jersey from extending its general state law benefits to all its citizens without regard to their religious belief." He then proceeded to his finding, after citing the police and fire protection, connections for sewage disposal and other public services, to that date at least deemed secular, which are provided to church-operated schools without question. "Of course, cutting off church schools from these services, so separate and so indisputably marked off from the religious function, would make it far more difficult for the schools to operate. But such is obviously not the purpose of the First Amendment. That Amendment requires the state to be a neutral in its relations with groups of religious believers and nonbelievers; it does not require the state to be their adversary. State power is no more to be used so as to handicap religions than it is to favor them. . . . The First Amendment has erected a wall between church and state. That wall must be kept high and impregnable. We could not approve the slightest breach. New Jersey has not breached it here."

Two dissenting opinions were filed in the case, one by Justice Jackson in which Justice Frankfurter joined, and one by Justice Rutledge, with whom Justices Frankfurter, Jackson, and Burton agreed. Justice Jackson took the full secularist viewpoint. "Our public school, if not a product of Protestantism, at least is more consistent with it than with the Catholic culture and scheme of values. It is a relatively recent development dating from about 1840. It is organized on the premise that secular education can be isolated from all religious teaching so that the school can inculcate all needed temporal knowledge and also maintain

a strict and lofty neutrality as to religion. The assumption
is that after the individual has been instructed in worldly
wisdom he will be better fitted to choose his religion.
Whether such a disjunction is possible, and if possible
whether it is wise, are questions I need not try to answer."
He then proceeded to argue that the majority ignored "the
essentially religious test by which beneficiaries of this expenditure are selected. A policeman protects a Catholic, of
course—but not because he is a Catholic; it is because he is
a man and a member of our society. The fireman protects
the Church school—but not because it is a Church school;
it is because it is property, part of the assets of our society.
. . . But before these school authorities draw a check to
reimburse for a student's fare they must ask just that question, and if the school is a Catholic one they may render aid
because it is such, while if it is of any other faith or is run
for profit, the help must be withheld."

Justices Burton and Rutledge did not join Justices Jackson
and Frankfurter in this opinion. The minority opinion in
which all four Justices joined was written by Justice Rutledge. Their viewpoint was compactly stated in two sen-
tences at the very start of the opinion: "Not simply an
established church, but any law respecting an establishment
of religion is forbidden. The Amendment was broadly but
not loosely phrased." There follows a history of the adoption of the First Amendment even longer than the incursion
into religious history that helped give a Janus-like quality to
the majority opinion. Thereafter the minority argument is
fairly compact. "Does New Jersey's action furnish support
for religion by use of the taxing power? Certainly it does, if
the test remains undiluted as Jefferson and Madison made
it, that money taken by taxation from one is not to be used
or given to support another's religious training or belief, or
indeed one's own." The cost of transportation, the minority
argued, is an essential part of the cost of education. In this

it does not differ from the payment of tuition, teachers' salaries, the construction costs of buildings and their equipment with the paraphernalia of education. "If the fact alone be determinative that religious schools are engaged in education, thus promoting the general and individual welfare, together with the legislature's decision that the payment of public moneys for their aid makes their work a public function, then I can see no possible basis, except one of dubious legislative policy, for the state's refusal to make full appropriation for support of private, religious schools, just as is done for public instruction. There could not be, on that basis, valid constitutional objection." Thus, on the *reductio ad absurdum* argument, the minority opinion concludes that since the cost of transportation is inseparable from the other costs of education, for the state legally to assume the burden of the former would imply the legal right, if not indeed the legal obligation, to support church schools in all their operating costs.

THE COST OF FREEDOM

The remainder of the minority opinion is largely devoted to the cost of freedom. The freedom to attend the church-supported school, which was established in the Pierce case, carries as its corollary the duty to assume all costs, direct and indirect, of religious-oriented education. "Like St. Paul's freedom, religious liberty with a great price must be bought. And for those who exercise it most fully, by insisting upon religious education for their children mixed with secular, by the terms of our Constitution the price is greater than for others." Nor would it suffice to treat the schools of all denominations alike. "It was the furnishing of 'contributions of money for the propagation of opinions which he disbelieves' that the fathers outlawed. That consequence

and effect are not removed by multiplying to all-inclusive-
ness the sects for which support is exacted. The Constitution
requires, not comprehensive identification of state with religion, but complete separation. . . ."

In many ways the presence of the new thinking that has
recently resulted in the banning of the Bible reading and
the recitation of the Lord's Prayer in classrooms is more
strikingly present in the majority opinion than in the Rutledge minority opinion. There is something to be said for
Justice Jackson's jibe: ". . . the undertones of the opinion,
advocating complete and uncompromising separation of
Church from State, seem utterly discordant with its conclusion yielding support to their commingling in educational
matters. The case which irresistibly comes to mind as the
most fitting precedent is that of Julia who, according to
Byron's reports, 'whispering "I will ne'er consent"—con-
sented.'" A comparison between the majority opinions in
the Louisiana textbook case and the New Jersey bus case
makes the point clear.

The court thinking in the Louisiana textbook case rested
upon a foundation with solid historic precedent. There is a
distinction among the People, the State, and the Church. If
a piece of legislation aids the People and the State but does
not aid the Church directly, it is constitutional. The free
loan of textbooks met these terms, therefore it was within
the competence of the Louisiana legislature. There can be
little doubt that in the thinking of the Supreme Court in
1930 a bus ride would be just as secular as a geography book.
A free bus ride for all school children would aid the people
and the state; a free bus ride would be constitutional.

But by 1947 the traditional distinction among the People,
the State, and the Church is ignored. The first and the third
are fused in contradistinction to the second, in the majority
opinion as well as in the minority. Out of this fusion emerges
the new pattern of thinking. Does the Constitution forbid an

establishment of religion, or does it forbid an establishment of *religion?* These subtleties are hard to grasp, and even harder to express on the printed page. A free bus ride is certainly not an *establishment* of religion; that phrase has a distinct historical meaning. But is any aid, however slight, however indirect, that may accrue to a church through social legislation designed to aid the people and the State an establishment of *religion?* The minority obviously thought so and obviously thought that that was what the Constitution forbade, but so did the majority. The only point at issue was whether the free bus ride aided the church through the church-supported school, although it was really designed to aid the parent who was reimbursed for the bus fare. The majority thought not, the minority thought so. The conclusion would seem to be that by 1947 the Supreme Court considered social legislation unconstitutional if a church received oblique assistance through it.

The Court in 1963 took the stand that "a strict and lofty neutrality as to religion" is the only spirit that can preserve the separation of Church and State in the public schools. The older doctrine, that the People, the State, and the Church are distinct entities and that social legislation may benefit the first two even though it obliquely benefits the third, is at least imperiled and may well be obsolete. And yet—the First Amendment has not changed its wording; the Fourteenth Amendment still carries the same guarantees it always carried. From 1871 until 1947 the Court was dedicated to the preservation of the religious rights of the minority. It has recently dedicated itself, with or without explicit intention, to the establishment of the religious rule of the minority. Such is the logical deduction from the opinions that prevailed in the Regents'-prayer case, the Bible-reading case and Lord's Prayer case.

This is a point to be established in the next chapter. The thesis underlying the present chapter is that beneath the

diversity in the opinions considered, there was the observa-
tion of a single principle, that the First Amendment as im-
plemented by the Fourteenth protects the religious rights
of minorities. In *Meyer* v. *Nebraska* and *Pierce* v. *Society
of Sisters* it was the right of religious minorities, the Lutherans of Nebraska who wished to send their children to
German-language schools and the Catholics of Oregon who
wished to send their children to parochial schools, to do so.
In *Cochran* v. *Louisiana State Board of Education* and
Everson v. *Board of Education* it was the right of minorities
attending church-operated schools to share in the benefits of
social legislation.

As Justice Jackson said in the Jehovah's Witnesses case, it
is the collisions between conflicting rights "which most frequently require intervention of the State to determine where
the rights of one end and those of another begin." No such
collision existed in the Nebraska and Oregon cases. The
right of the minority to send their children to church-operated schools in no way conflicts with the right of the majority to send their children to public schools. In the Jehovah's Witnesses cases at least the possibility of such collision
exists. In the Gobitis case the Court not only found that
there was a collision but ruled that "the promotion of national cohesion" through a compulsory flag salute was more
important than respect for the religious scruples of the
Witnesses. But this opinion ran counter to an opinion that
had been gradually building up since 1871, that the Fourteenth Amendment protected the religious rights of minorities from infringement by the states. When the Court
reversed itself in the Barnette opinion, it returned to the
main pattern of thinking. The Louisiana textbook case and
the New Jersey bus case brought in another potential conflict, that between the beneficiaries of social legislation and
the pocketbook of the taxpayer. The Court simply did not
allow this conflict to develop; to do so would have raised

a question about the constitutional validity of all social legislation. The difference between the two opinions lay in the fact that in 1930 the Court was satisfied with the constitutionality of social legislation that aided the People and the State, and might be thought only incidentally to have aided the Church. In 1947 this was no longer true. There is certainly no visible difference between a free textbook and a free bus ride as devices of social legislation. But the incidental aid to a church loomed so large in 1947 that four of the nine justices considered it the compelling consideration and the other five considered it a matter worthy of detailed consideration. In short, by 1947 the Court was about ready to maintain that aid to a church, even when oblique, incidental, and virtually accidental, is unconstitutional.

14

Minority Rule

In all the cases considered in the preceding chapter there was a common denominator, the protection of the religious rights of minorities. They might be rights the exercise of which involved no possible conflict with majority rights, as in the Nebraska and Oregon private school cases; they might be rights the exercise of which involved possible conflict with the basic social rights as in the Jehovah's Witnesses cases, or pedestrian pocketbook rights as in the Louisiana textbook and New Jersey bus cases. In every case considered, the point at issue was the preservation of the religious rights of a minority. There was never any question of the limitation of the rights of the majority.

But with the opinions, both majority and minority, in the New Jersey bus case, a new and still undetermined factor entered the equation. At the risk of over-simplification it might be said that all cases prior to the New Jersey bus case were settled by the extension to the states through the Fourteenth Amendment of the second religion clause of the First Amendment, "Congress shall make no law . . . prohibiting the free exercise thereof." But this clause obviously was inapplicable in the case of the free bus ride for the parochial school child. A taxpayer's suit of the ordinary sort, decided on the due-process phrase in a case of social legislation, would open a Pandora's box of woes. The logical, or at least the legalistic, result was that the case really was settled on the first clause, 'Congress shall make no law respecting an establishment of religion. . . .'

We attempted in the preceding chapter to suggest by italics a distinction that is profound and yet difficult to draw, the distinction between an *establishment* of religion and an establishment of *religion*. When the word *establishment* is italicized, the phrase has a definite historical meaning. An establishment is a state-supported church; historically a synonym for the Church of England has been The Establishment. But when the word *religion* is italicized, then an undetermined and indeterminable swarm of implications, inferences, corollaries, and conclusions emerges from the philological cocoon. They began to emerge in 1948, in the McCollum case. This case involved released time for the religious instruction of public school children.

A bit of public school definition may be in order here. The term *released time* is ordinarily applied to the practice of conducting religious instruction within the school building. When it is conducted outside, it is called *dismissed time*. The McCollum case was a released-time case. The Zorach case, which bears a relationship to it similar to the relationship of the Barnette case to the Gobitis case in the Jehovah's Witnesses series, was a dismissed-time case.

RELEASED TIME

The history of released time in American public education began in 1914 and ended in 1948. It started in Gary, Indiana, where the superintendent of schools, Dr. William Wirt, believed that the moral and ethical standards of a youthful generation reared in the shadow of the steel mills needed a light steadier and clearer than their lurid fires. The belief of Dr. Wirt was shared by many, and the Gary plan of released time for religious instruction caught on. Before long it developed its logical offspring, dismissed time, whereby the religious instruction was given off premises. The next development was to give school credit for courses of Bible study, and Alvin Johnson reported that in 1927 twenty-five states did.[1] No one seems to have suspected that the Constitution of the United States was being violated.

Twenty more years passed before that suspicion became rife even in terms of state constitutions. In 1947 a California court upheld a statute which allowed students to be excused from their regular classes to attend religious classes (*Gordon* v. *Board of Education of City of Los Angeles,* 178 *Pacific Reporter* 488). Two years later the New York court of appeals did the same (*People ex rel. Lewis* v. *Spalding,* 299 N.Y. 564). Then came the McCollum case.

In 1946 an Illinois court had sustained the constitutionality of the state's released-time law (*People ex rel. Latimer et al.* v. *Board of Education of the City of Chicago,* 394 Ill. 228). Mrs. Vashti McCollum, wife of a University of Illinois professor and described as a "rationalist," decided to try again. Champaign, the university town, had a released-time program organized in 1940 by the Champaign Council on Religious Education by members of the Catholic, Jewish, and Protestant faiths. For eight years Protestant teachers, Catholic priests, and a Jewish rabbi conducted released-time classes, although the Jewish class was discontinued before 1948. Classes were conducted in the classrooms of the public schools; attendance was voluntary on the request of parents, students participating were excused for the thirty or forty-five minutes involved each week. Attendance was checked and reported to the public school teachers.

Those not participating in the program carried on their secular studies.

Mrs. McCollum had a son in the Champaign schools. She brought suit, alleging that the program expended public funds for sectarian activities, denied the equal protection of the laws, and violated state and federal guarantees of the freedom of religion. The Chicago Civil Liberties Committee backed her up. The circuit court, in denying a writ of mandamus, found "there is nothing in any expression of the Federal Supreme Court that remotely indicates that there is any constitutional objection to the Champaign plan of religious education," and the Illinois supreme court unanimously affirmed its finding (396 Ill. 14). In October 1947 Mrs. McCollum carried the case to the Supreme Court, with the American Civil Liberties Union sharing the burden.

The Supreme Court reversed the Illinois courts in an eight-to-one opinion, Justice Reed dissenting. Justice Black wrote the majority opinion. He defined the case as one relating "to the power of a state to utilize its tax-supported public school system in aid of religious instruction insofar as that power may be restricted by the First and Fourteenth Amendments to the Federal Constitution (*Illinois ex rel. McCollum* v. *Board of Education,* 333 U.S. 203). After outlining the background of the case he stated, "This is beyond all question a utilization of the tax-established and tax-supported public school system to aid religious groups and to spread their faith. And it falls squarely under the ban of the First Amendment (made applicable to the States by the Fourteenth) as we interpreted it in *Everson* v. *Board of Education,* 330 U.S. 1. . . ." He then turned to the defense argument, which rested on two premises—that the First Amendment was intended to forbid only governmental preference for one religion over another and not governmental assistance for all religions, and that the Fourteenth Amendment did not make the establishment-of-religion clause of the First applicable to the states. Both contentions he rejected without refutation. After stating that no hostility to religion was intended in his opinion, he concluded, ". . . the First Amendment rests upon the premise that both religion and government can best work to achieve their lofty aims if each is left free from the other within their respective spheres. Or, as we said in the Everson case, the First Amendment has erected a wall between Church and State which must be kept high and impregnable. Here not only are the State's tax-supported public school buildings used for the dissemination of religious doctrine. The State also affords sectarian groups an invaluable aid in that it helps to provide pupils for their religious classes through use of the State's compulsory public school machinery. This is not separation of Church and State."

Justice Frankfurter filed a collateral opinion in which he was joined by Justices Burton, Jackson, and Rutledge. After pointing out that "the meaning of a spacious conception like that of the separation of Church from State is unfolded as appeal is made to the principle from case to case," he proceeded to a brief outline of the historical relationship between education and religion. Historically they have been closely related, the close relationship continued in colonial America, but he maintained that this ceased to be true in the United States. After citing the slow dissociation of education and religion in Virginia, New York, and Massachusetts, he stated, "The upshot of these controversies, often long and fierce, is fairly summarized by saying that long before the Fourteenth Amendment subjected the States to new limitations, the prohibition of furtherance by the State of religious instruction became the guiding principle, in law and feeling, of the American people. . . . Separation in the field of education, then, was not imposed upon unwilling States by force of superior law. In this respect the Fourteenth Amendment merely reflected a principle then dominant in our national life. To the extent that the Constitution thus made it binding upon the States, the basis of the restriction is the whole experience of our people." The remainder of his opinion is largely devoted to the assurance that the viewpoint expressed does not imply hostility to religion but rather is motivated by the desire to reconcile religious freedom with general freedom. One aspect of his opinion was prophetic of the finding in the Zorach case. He stated, "We do not consider as indeed we could not, school programs not before us which, though colloquially characterized as 'released time,' present situations differing in aspects that may well be constitutionally crucial. Different forms which 'released time' has taken during more than thirty years of growth include programs which, like that before us, would not withstand the test of the constitution; others may be found unexceptional."

A very curious opinion was expressed by Justice Jackson. He was uncertain that anyone's freedom was curtailed by the Champaign released-time plan; he held that the Constitution protected no one "from the embarrassment that always attends non-conformity, whether in religion, politics, behavior, or dress"; he could see no ground for a finding based on the due-process clause, since "any cost of this plan to the taxpayers is incalculable and negligible"; he doubted the wisdom of excluding all religious instruction from the schools; he felt that the majority opinion was too far-reaching—and he agreed with the majority. It might be plausibly argued that he made out as strong a case for dissent as did Justice Reed, who dissented.

Justice Reed, in his dissent, found himself unable to determine the precise aspect of the Champaign plan which the majority found unconstitutional: "From the tenor of the opinions I conclude that their teachings are that any use of a pupil's school time, whether that use is on or off the school grounds, with the necessary school regulations to facilitate attendance, falls under the ban. . . ." He then turned, as had Justice Frankfurter, to history and found that Thomas Jefferson, as rector of the University of Virginia for which Madison was one of the visitors, had established a system of released time at the university. He also found Madison's *Memorial and Remonstrance against Religious Assessments* not applicable, since its subject was establishment in the historical sense of the word. He cited the substantial aid religion receives from the State in the form of freedom from taxation, the court judgments in the Louisiana textbook case and the New Jersey bus case, the precedent of *Bradfield* v. *Roberts* (175 U.S. 291) in which the Court held it constitutional for the federal government to finance an addition to a hospital chartered to a religious order. He instanced the chaplains who invoke the divine blessing at each daily meeting of Congress, the commissioned chaplains in the armed forces, the compulsory attendance at church services at West Point and Annapolis.

He concluded eloquently, "The prohibition of enactments respecting the establishment of religion does not bar every friendly gesture between church and state. It is not an absolute prohibition against every conceivable situation where the two may work together, any more than the other provisions of the First Amendment—free speech, free press—are absolutes. . . . This Court cannot be too cautious in upsetting practices embedded in our society by many years of experience. A state is entitled to have great leeway in its legislation when dealing with the important social problems of its population. A definite violation of legislative limits must be established. The Constitution should not be stretched to forbid national customs in the way courts act to reach arrangements to avoid federal taxation. Devotion to the great principle of religious liberty should not lead us into a rigid interpretation of the constitutional guarantee that conflicts with accepted habits of our people. This is an instance where, for me, the history of past practices is determinative of the meaning of a constitutional clause, not a decorous introduction to the study of its text. The judgment should be affirmed."

Justice Black stated in the majority opinion that at Champaign the public schools were being used to aid religious groups to spread their faith. This was unquestionably true, since the religious classes were held in public school classrooms. He stated that this fell squarely under the ban of the First Amendment as made applicable to the states by the Fourteenth and as so interpreted in the Everson case. The part of the majority opinion in the Everson case to which he probably referred states, "Neither a state nor the Federal government can set up a church. Neither can pass laws which aid one religion, aid all religions, or prefer one religion over another." The Champaign plan undoubtedly aided all religions whose members chose to avail themselves of it. One can sympathize, however, with Justice Reed who found it "difficult to extract from the opinions any conclusion as to what it is in the Champaign plan that is unconstitutional. . . . None of the reversing opinions say whether the purpose of the Champaign plan for religious instruction during school hours is unconstitutional or whether it is some ingredient used in or omitted from the formula that makes the plan unconstitutional. From the tenor of the opinions I conclude that their teachings are that any use of a pupil's school time, whether that use is on or off the school grounds, with the necessary school regulations to facilitate attendance, falls under the ban. . . ."

On the whole, the separate opinion of Justice Frankfurter is more useful for the light it sheds on majority thinking. He held that a spacious concept such as the separation of Church and State unfolds as appeal is made from case to case. He maintained that long before the Fourteenth Amendment subjected the states to new limitations, the prohibition of furtherance by a state of religious instruction became the guiding principle, in law and feeling, of the American people and hence, in this respect, the Fourteenth Amendment merely reflected a principle then dominant in our national life.

But is this exactly true? There was a growing opposition evidenced for many decades against sectarian religious teaching in the public schools. Conversely there was a growing sentiment in favor of nonsectarian teaching. Perhaps non-sectarian religious teaching is a theological impossibility, and very likely it is a practical impossibility in a pluralistic society. But *non-sectarian* is not a synonym for *secular*. In practice there was an enormous amount of non-sectarian religious teaching in the schools which aimed at inculcating something like a common denominator of Protestant belief, both before and long after the passage of the Fourteenth Amendment. Furthermore, the acceptance of the Gary released-time plan by other communities and the fact that it went legally unchallenged for about three decades indicate that there was no substantial opposition to sectarian teaching in school buildings, provided the sects were separated. The Gary released-time plan was based on two premises: first, that children needed religious instruction, and parents wanted them to have it; second, that there is no such thing as meaningful non-sectarian religious teaching in a society so pluralistic as the American.

It is not our purpose, however, to argue that Justice Reed was right and the rest were wrong in the McCollum finding. Our sole purpose is to point out that for the first time in a religious-freedom case, the Court ruled that the viewpoint of a minority should prevail over the will of the majority. That a majority of people in Champaign and other communities with released-time programs favored them can hardly be disputed; substantial opposition to any program in the public schools never stays mute. Thus the McCollum case differed basically from all the cases considered in the last chapter. In the cases that started with the Nebraska foreign-language school case and concluded with the New Jersey bus case, the rights of minorities were affirmed but not at the expense of what the majority wanted. Whether explicitly or implicitly, every case in this series was settled on the second religion clause of the First Amendment, which prohibits Congress to make a law ". . . prohibiting the free exercise thereof." It might be a matter of direct free exercise as in the Oregon parochial school case or extremely oblique free exercise as in the New Jersey bus case, but in each of these cases the second clause of the amendment prevailed and a minority right was protected. But in the McCollum case the finding was based, as indeed it would have to be, on the first clause, which states, "Congress shall make no law respecting an establishment of religion. . . ." In the majority opinion the term *establishment* lost its historical meaning and took on its everyday, twentieth-century meaning. The net result was a finding that denied the majority what for some thirty and more years it had regarded as its unquestionable right. That the majority felt itself deprived of something precious and perhaps felt its rights threatened with further invasion was made crystal-clear by the tumult and the shouting that followed the McCollum verdict. The cynic may say that the result was the Zorach verdict. The historian contents himself with saying that the Zorach verdict followed the McCollum.

Dismissed Time

The Zorach case arose out of the New York Education Law. This statute allows schools to dismiss pupils for religious instruction given outside the school building and financed entirely by the churches participating. Students not dismissed for religious instruction stay in school and continue their everyday studies. The constitutionality of the statute was challenged and the case reached the New York Court of Appeals in 1949, which upheld its constitutionality (*People ex rel. Lewis* v. *Spalding*, 299 N.Y. 564). It was then appealed to the Supreme Court, which, in 1952, upheld the New York finding. The majority opinion was delivered by Justice Douglas.

After outlining the New York plan of dismissed-time religious instruction, Justice Douglas denied that it resembled the Champaign released-time program, since the religious instruction was not given in public school classrooms and there was no expenditure of public funds. He then came to grips with the appellant's fundamental argument, that the weight of school authority was placed behind religious instruction and thus an element of coercion existed that amounted to an establishment of religion. The majority opinion denied categorically that there was any evidence in the record to support the claim of coercion. "The present record indeed tells us that the school authorities are neutral in this regard and do no more than release students whose parents so request. If in fact coercion were used, if it were established that any one or more teachers were using their office to persuade or force students to take the religious instruction, a wholly different case would be presented. Hence we put aside that claim of coercion both as respects the 'free exercise' of religion and 'an establishment of religion' within the meaning of the First Amendment" (*Zorach* v. *Clauson*, 343 U.S. 306).

Then came the most significant part of the opinion, and the part that marked a retreat from the salient established in the McCollum case. In that case Justice Black had proclaimed the doctrine of total separation of Church and State. It was that declaration of doctrine far more than the actual decision in the McCollum case that had evoked the storm of protest which swept the nation. In the Zorach case Justice Douglas, speaking for the majority, said, "There cannot be the slightest doubt that the First Amendment reflects the philosophy that Church and State should be separated. And so far as interference with the 'free exercise' of religion and an 'establishment' of religion are concerned, the separation must be complete and unequivocal. The First Amendment within the scope of its coverage permits no exception; the prohibition is absolute. The First Amendment, however, does not say that in every and all respects there shall be a separation of Church and State. Rather, it studiously defines the manner, the specific ways, in which there shall be no concert or union or dependence one on the other. That is the common sense of the matter. Otherwise the state and religion would be aliens to each other—hostile, suspicious, and even unfriendly."

There followed a catalogue of the absurdities to which the doctrine of total separation could lead: no police or fire protection for religious groups, no prayer in legislative halls, no Thanksgiving Day, no "so help me God" in courtrooms, no request that "God save the United States and this Honorable Court." And then, speaking solemnly for the majority, he said, "We are a religious people whose institutions presuppose a Supreme Being. . . . When the state encourages religious instruction or cooperates with religious authorities by adjusting the schedule of public events to sectarian needs, it follows the best of our traditions. For it then respects the religious nature of our people and accommodates the public service to their spiritual needs. To hold that it may not would be to find in the Constitution a requirement that the government show a callous indifference to religious groups. That would be preferring those who believe in no religion over those who do believe. . . . But we find no constitutional requirement which makes it necessary for government to be hostile to religion and to throw its weight against efforts to widen the effective scope of religious influence."

Not all the Justices were ready to follow Justice Douglas out of the salient. Justice Black, who had delivered the majority decision in the McCollum case, could see no difference between the Champaign and New York situations except the use of school buildings for religious instruction in the former and not in the latter. To him it was a difference without a distinction. But he made it clear that he dissented on broadly philosophic grounds. "In dissenting today, I mean to do more than give routine approval to our McCollum decision. I mean also to reaffirm my faith in the fundamental philosophy expressed in McCollum and *Everson* v. *Board of Education*. . . ." Thus his stand for the principle of total separation of Church and State remained unaltered.

Justice Frankfurter, in a separate opinion, also dissented but placed his emphasis primarily on the divisive influence of a dismissed-time program. Justice Jackson, in his dissent, believed that coercion was present in New York and that "The day this country ceases to be free for irreligion it will cease to be free for religion—except for the sect that can win political power. The same epithetical jurisprudence used by the Court today to beat down those who oppose pressuring children into some religion can devise as good epithets tomorrow against those who object to pressuring them into a favored religion. And after all, if we concede to the State power and wisdom to single out 'duly constituted religious' bodies as exclusive alternatives for compulsory secular instruction, it would be logical to also uphold the power and wisdom to choose the true faith among those 'duly constituted.' We start down a rough road when we begin to mix compulsory public education with compulsory godliness. . . ."

Had the Zorach finding followed the McCollum precedent, the storm of protest that the latter elicited might have seemed a benign zephyr compared to the tornado of protest that the former would have set whirling. Again the rights of the majority were basically at stake. Released-time programs never were so common as dismissed-time programs. Most school boards, and no doubt most Americans, felt that there was something inappropriate in the use of public school classrooms for religious instruction. This feeling was not extended to off-premises instruction on school time. Hence the dismissed-time program was, and is, the common one. The outlawed released-time program never was common.

We say that the rights of the majority were basically at stake. At this point it might be well to spell out specifically the thinking, however vague and unphilosophic it may be in the average person's mind, about education. To the average American the formal education of his child is part of the rearing of his child. He is not prepared to undertake that education himself, and so he lets out the job to someone else. In most cases the someone else is the school system of his community. But he thinks of that school system as his agent, acting in his interest and under his supervisory direction. He elects a school board to represent him in the supervision, and he attends PTA meetings to make more effective his interest. But when he thinks of himself as being in the last analysis the owner of that system, he does so not as a taxpayer but as a parent. He can allocate the education of his child to a secular agent, but he cannot surrender his education to it. He cannot surrender it because, as he sees it, that education is part of his God-given duty and he cannot render to Caesar, except as his agent, the things that are God's. When he asks, "What right has the Supreme Court to say how my child shall be educated?" he does not mean what legal right but what moral right. He feels that moral rights arise from moral duties, and are not in the power of the Supreme Court to give or withhold.

There can be little doubt that thinking of this sort lay behind the majority opinion in the Zorach case. Had Justice Douglas so spelled it out, the service to American society would have been enormous. To talk of the total separation of Church and State is to talk of something that cannot be on sea or land because the same human beings comprise both. There has always been at least one voice on the Supreme Court to say this, and twice in recent history that voice finally prevailed. It was the voice of Justice Stone in the Gobitis case, and he prevailed three years later. It was the voice of Justice Reed in the McCollum case, and he prevailed four years later. It was the voice of Justice Stewart in the Regents'-prayer case and the Bible-reading case. But at this point the historian resolutely limits himself to history. But even as he does so, he remembers that history is first cousin to prophecy.

SUNDAY OBSERVANCE

Another bit of the salient was cut off in the cases involving Sunday-observance laws. Every state except Alaska has some sort of Sunday-observance law, but only a quarter of the states exempt Orthodox Jews and Seventh-Day Adventists as conscientious Sabbatarians. In 1960 the Supreme Court faced a situation in which the federal court of the first circuit had declared the Massachusetts Sunday-observance law unconstitutional and the federal court of the third circuit had declared its almost identical twin in Pennsylvania constitutional. Judge Calvert Magruder, speaking for the majority in a divided court, found the Massachusetts law essentially a religious statute and hence an establishment of religion. Judge William Hastie, delivering the opinion of the third circuit court, concluded that the refusal of the Supreme Court in 1951 to review the New York Sunday-observance law established the comparable absence of a substantial federal question in the Pennsylvania statute. Then the two cases along with a similar one from Maryland came to the Supreme Court.

Justice Warren delivered the opinion of the majority. He conceded the religious origin of the Sunday statutes but held that their 1960 basis was no longer exclusively, or even primarily, religious. He stated, ". . . the State's purpose is not merely to provide a one-day-in-seven work stoppage. In addition to this, the State seeks to set one day apart from all the others as a day of rest, repose, recreation and tranquillity—a day which all members of the family and community have the opportunity to spend and enjoy together . . ." (*McGowan* v. *Maryland*, 362 U.S. 959). In other words, although the statutes may provide incidental benefit to religion, their primary purpose is social. The finding represented a clear return to the thinking that prevailed thirty years before in the Louisiana textbook case and another rejection of the doctrine of total separation of Church and State. Justice Warren made this abundantly clear when he said, ". . . if the State regulates conduct by enacting a general law within its power, the purpose and effect of which is to advance the State's secular goals, the statute is valid despite its indirect burden on religious observance unless the State may accomplish its purpose by means which do not impose such a burden."

And yet the cases are not entirely parallel. In the Louisiana case the Court affirmed the right of a minority to share in the benefits of social legislation despite some incidental benefit to religion. In the Sunday Law case the Court affirmed the right of the majority to enjoy the benefits of social legislation despite some incidental injury to the minority resulting from a conflict with their religious convictions. It is presumably not without significance that dissents from the majority opinion were filed by justices with a record of careful consideration for religious rights, Justices Douglas, Brennan, and Stewart. If the Zorach decision illustrates the wisdom of rejecting the doctrine of complete separation of Church and State, the McGowan decision illustrates its difficulties. To deny majority rights as a means of protecting minority rights is bad government. To protect equally majority and minority rights when they provide an area of conflict is good government. It has never been claimed that good government is easy. The McGowan decision was a necessary guarantee of majority rights, as truly as was the Zorach decision. But the problem of accommodating to it the rights of Sabbatarians stays unsolved, except to the extent that the feedom from the Sunday sales ban on Sabbatarians provided in ten states comprises an accommodation. Sufficient accommodation is a legislative imperative for the several states, but it is not an accommodation to be achieved at the expense of majority rights. The observance of minority rights does not imply the necessity of accepting minority rule.

THE REGENTS'-PRAYER CASE

There remain to be considered the three religious-exercise cases, the case that centered about the prayer recommended for school recital by the New York State Board of Regents and the cases involving the reading of the Bible and the recitation of the Lord's Prayer in public schools. All three differ in a basic respect from the McCollum case, but all three were settled on the principle enunciated in the New Jersey bus case and applied in the McCollum case. The reading of the Bible or the recital of a prayer is a religious exercise, not a form of religious instruction. Religious instruction in public school classrooms was barred by the McCollum decision. Religious exercises were barred by the three more recent decisions.

In 1951 the New York State Board of Regents, which has general supervisory charge of public education in the Empire State, recommended that the school day be opened by the pledge of allegiance to the flag and by the recital of the following prayer: "Almighty God, we acknowledge our dependence upon Thee, and we beg Thy blessings upon us, our parents, our teachers, and our country." This simple statement was the end product of a long deliberation in which representatives of many religious denominations participated. It was intended as a prayer that might be said by all who believe in a personal God and in the dependence of man upon Him. Its legality was tested by parents of pupils in the New Hyde Park District and upheld by the state courts. In 1957 the prayer was adopted by the North Hempstead Board of Education and again its legality challenged. This time an appeal was made to the Supreme Court from the affirmative finding of the state courts. The Supreme Court held it unconstitutional in a six-to-one divided opinion. Justice Frankfurter, who was ill, and Justice White, who received his court appointment subsequent to the hearing of the case, did not participate. Justice Black, who delivered the majority opinion in McCollum and refused to budge from the position then taken when the Zorach case was tried, again delivered the majority opinion. Chief Justice Warren and Justices Brennan, Clark, and Harlan joined him, Justice Potter Stewart dissenting.

The basic argument of the majority was that the prayer violated the no-establishment clause, since "that prayer was composed by governmental officials as part of a governmental program to further religious beliefs" (*Engel* v. *Vitale*, 370 U.S. 421). That participation in the prayer was voluntary and that the prayer might be considered "denominationally neutral" were not considered palliatives. The majority also harkened back to the coercive factor it considered to be present here as it had been considered to be present in McCollum and, by the minority, in Zorach. Justice Black stated, "When the power, prestige and financial support of government is placed behind a particular religious belief, the indirect coercive pressure upon religious minorities to conform to the prevailing officially approved religion is plain." Justice Black was careful to dissociate the Regents' prayer from other documents containing references to the Deity such as the Declaration of Independence and the National Anthem. His point was that the recital of the Regents' prayer was a religious exercise, the singing of "The Star-Spangled Banner" a patriotic one. He concluded with the assurance that the decision was not anti-religious.

Justice Douglas, who concurred with the majority, filed a separate opinion in which he stressed a belief that the true crux was the expenditure of public funds for the maintenance of the program, the expenditure presumably being the minuscule proportion of the teachers' salary paid for the moment that it took to recite the prayer. "The point for decision is whether the government can constitutionally finance a religion"; maintaining that the government is "honeycombed with such financing," he stated, "I think it is an unconstitutional undertaking whatever form it takes." He was less impressed by the argument of coercion which he felt was present in McCollum, conceded that to authorize the prayer was not "to establish a religion in the strictly historic meaning of the words," but did fear the divisive influence of such a religious exercise. Probably the most significant statement that he made was a reversal of his opinion in the New Jersey bus case. "The Everson case seems in retrospect to be out of line with the First Amendment. Its result is appealing, as it allows aid to be given to needy children. Yet by the same token, public funds could be used to satisfy other needs of children in parochial schools— lunches, books, and tuition being obvious examples." Thus in the sense that he stressed the expenditure of public funds, Justice Douglas based his opinion on a narrower base than did his associates in the majority opinion; in the sense that he would now determine the right of school children to participate in social legislation by the schools they attend, he broadened it.

The minority opinion was filed by Justice Stewart. It followed the customary pattern of thought of those who oppose the attempt to effect a total separation of Church and State. He could not see how "letting those who want to say a prayer say it" was establishing an "official religion." He believed that the Court would be wise to place smaller stress on the history of religious strife in England and more on the traditions of America. He cited the references to the Deity in the National Anthem and the Pledge of Allegiance, and observed that no one had challenged as unconstitutional the National Day of Prayer enacted by Congress in 1952. He pointed out that the chaplains in the armed services are paid from the public treasury as are the chaplains in penal institutions. He maintained that such prayer programs recognize and follow "the deeply entrenched and highly cherished spiritual traditions of our nation—traditions which come down to us from those who almost two hundred years ago avowed in the Declaration of Independence their 'firm reliance on the protection of divine providence' when they proclaimed the freedom and independence of this brave new world."

The reaction to the Engel case followed the easily predictable pattern: those who could be expected to approve did so, and those who could be expected to disapprove did so. Whichever viewpoint was right, in so far as there is a right viewpoint in such matters, one fact is incontestable: once more, in a clash between majority rights and minority rights, the Supreme Court had issued a decision which favored the latter at the expense of the former. The practice of opening school with a prayer is a time-hallowed American custom, although statutory provision for it is relatively recent. The reading of a Bible passage is a derivative of it, a first concession to non-sectarianism in the root meaning of the word. The recital of such a prayer as that sponsored by the Board of Regents was a second concession; the prayer usually said has been the Lord's Prayer. One may safely assume that the New Testament connotations of the Lord's Prayer would suggest sectarian considerations to many New Yorkers. Generations of Americans have considered it right to open the school day with a prayer. In their perhaps unphilosophic way, such Americans would consider what is right to be their right.

Every effort was made in New York to adapt what was considered a traditional American right to the mid-twentieth-century situation in the state. The churches of the state were broadly represented in the composition of the prayer. It was limited in its theological foundation to the expression of a belief in God and a belief that human welfare was His concern. It represented, as well as human care could achieve, a non-sectarian common denominator of religious belief. It did affirm, however, a belief in God and in His providence. This belief conflicted with a minority belief. The Supreme Court ruled the saying of the prayer unconstitutional. The minority had had the right not to say it, but in the view of the Court that was not enough. The Engel decision again translated a minority right into minority rule.

The argument based on coercion illustrates the fact. There was no charge of direct coercion. The charge involved the sort of indirect and subtle coercion exercised by the example of the majority upon a minority presumably lacking in the moral courage to be different. In so far as the thinking of the Court majority was influenced by the coercion argument, it was to resolve the conflict between a traditional majority right and a minority right in favor of the latter to the exclusion of the former.

Would such a resolution be a matter of principle with the Court? Let us assume the situation reversed. Let us assume a community in which secular humanists comprise the majority. It has been their tradition to open the school day without prayer. Into the community come some children of religious background accustomed to the opening of the school day with prayer. The absence of prayer would be a subtle, indirect coercion upon their belief that the school day should open with prayer. The absence of prayer would be a divisive force between this religious-minded minority and the secular-minded majority. Would the Supreme Court find the absence of prayer under such circumstances unconstitutional since it inhibited the free exercise of religion and was a coercive and divisive force?

It seems to the writer that any argument based on alleged coercive and divisive forces is at the very best a weak reed on which to lean. One can understand the argument that any intrusion of religion, in any form including the mere repetition of a religious formula like "So help me God," can be considered a violation of the no-establishment clause, although one retains the right to think that that interpretation is as nonsensical as it is unhistoric. One finds it very difficult indeed to understand the reasoning of a Court, which has frequently stressed the danger of violation to religious freedom on the part of government, when it uses the argument of coercion and division as a grounds for denying to the majority what has been in its tradition one of its cherished rights. Certainly it is no less coercion when applied to the majority by the judicial branch, and if the all-healing balm of abstention from prayer has healed the divisions present in New York as in every state in the nation and every nation on earth, the record in the daily press does not reveal it.

BIBLE READING AND THE LORD'S PRAYER

The Court decision in the Bible-reading and Lord's Prayer cases followed logically from the pattern of thinking evidenced from the New Jersey bus case through the Regents'-prayer case. Since a single decision covered both cases and since the same set of arguments underlay it, the cases can be considered together. Their factual backgrounds, of course, are different.

The Bible-reading case was initiated in Abington Township, Pennsylvania, by Edward and Sidney Schempp, who have been stated to be Unitarians. They contended that the state law which required the daily reading of at least ten Bible verses without comment was unconstitutional, as was the local practice of adding to it the recitation of the Lord's Prayer. The federal district court upheld the Schempp contention, ruling that the Pennsylvania Bible-reading program was both an establishment of religion and an infringement on the free exercise of religion (*Schempp* v. *Abington School District*, 177 Federal Supplement 298). In the light of this decision the Pennsylvania General Assembly changed the law, making the Bible reading discretionary rather than mandatory. The Supreme Court, to which appeal had been made, remanded the case to the district court in the light of this change in the law. The case was retired in the district court with the same result as before. The case was then carried once more to the Supreme Court, and in June 1963, Justice Clark delivered the majority opinion which sustained the Pennsylvania district court judgment.

The Lord's Prayer case was initiated in Baltimore, Maryland, by Mrs. Madalyn Murray and her son William J. Murray III, who are described in the majority opinion as "professed atheists." In 1905 the board of school commissioners of Baltimore adopted a rule requiring the reading, without comment, of a chapter of the Bible at the start of each school day, which might or might not be accompanied by the recitation of the Lord's Prayer. Mrs. Murray and her son contended that the requirement was unconstitutional, but the Maryland Court of Appeals, in a four-to-three decision, held that the requirement did not violate the Constitution. The case then was carried to the Supreme Court.

Justice Clark, who delivered the majority opinion, first outlined in substantial detail the background of the Schempp case and then briefly the background of the Murray case. He next proceeded to a recognition of the place of religion in American life, followed by a resumé of the Everson, Zorach, and Engel cases. Then came his enunciation of the principle upon which the finding ultimately rested: "What are the purpose and the primary effect of the enactment? If either is the advancement or inhibition of religion then the enactment exceeds the scope of legislative power as circumscribed by the Constitution. That is to say that to withstand the strictures of the establishment clause there must be a secular legislative purpose and a primary effect that neither advances nor inhibits religion." Next he pointed to a distinction drawn in the Engel case: ". . . a violation of the free exercise clause is predicated on coercion while the establishment clause need not be so attended." Recognizing that coercion need not be established as a factor essential to a violation of the no-establishment clause, he maintained that the reading of the Bible and the recitation of the Lord's Prayer were religious exercises prescribed as classroom activities. "Given that finding, the exercises and the law requiring them are in violation of the establishment clause."

The place of the Bible in literary and historic studies he considered unchallenged. But he also considered that the position of the Bible in the literature of religion and the sectarian nature of its message when the message was read for itself and not obliquely for its literary and historic value were equally beyond challenge. Hence the reading of the Bible, like the recitation of the Lord's Prayer which one might assume also to be a literary and historic document, was unconstitutional when such required reading was designed as a religious exercise.

For the first time in the series of cases initiated by the Everson decision a majority opinion considered the possible infringement of majority rights. Late in his opinion Justice Clark stated, "Finally, we cannot accept that the concept of neutrality which does not permit a state to require a religious exercise even with the consent of the majority of those affected, collides with the majority's right to free exercise of religion. While the free exercise clause clearly prohibits the use of state action to deny the rights of free exercise to anyone, it has never meant that a majority could use the machinery of the state to practice beliefs." The opinion then proceeds to what has become the time-hallowed recognition in such documents: "The place of religion in our society is an exalted one. . . ."

Justice Brennan, who concurred in the majority opinion, was sufficiently disturbed by the possible connotation of the finding that the Court was outlawing "every vestige of cooperation, however slight, between religion and government" that he filed a separate 25,000-word concurring opinion. "Our decision in these cases does not clearly forecast anything about the constitutionality of other types of interdependence between religious and other institutions," he maintained. "What the Framers meant to foreclose, and what our decisions under the Establishment Clause have forbidden, are those involvements of religious with secular institutions which (a) serve the essentially religious activities of religious institutions; (b) employ the organs of government for essentially religious purposes; or (c) use essentially religious means to serve governmental ends, when secular means would suffice."

Again, as in the Engel case, Justice Stewart dissented. After calling attention to what he considered the deficiencies in the records of the two cases, he said, "It is, I think, a fallacious oversimplification to regard these two provisions [the religion clauses of the First Amendment] as establishing a single constitutional standard of 'separation of church and state,' which can be mechanically applied in every case to delineate the required boundaries between government and religion. We err in the first place if we do not recognize, as a matter of history and as a matter of the imperatives of our free society, that religion and government must necessarily interact in countless ways. Secondly, the fact is that while in many contexts the establishment clause and the free exercise clause fully complement each other, there are areas in which a doctrinaire reading of the establishment clause leads to irreconcilable conflict with the free exercise clause."

Justice Stewart then proceeded to point out a historic aspect of the First Amendment previously overlooked in these opinions which relied in part upon the appeal to history. "As a matter of history, the First Amendment was adopted solely as a limitation upon the newly created national government. The events leading to its adoption strongly suggest that the establishment clause was primarily an attempt to insure that Congress not only would be powerless to establish a national church, but would also be unable to interfere with existing state establishments. . . . Each state was left free to go its own way and pursue its own policy with respect to religion. . . . I accept too the proposition that the Fourteenth Amendment has somehow absorbed the establishment clause, although it is not without irony that a constitutional provision evidently designed to leave the states free to go their own way should now have become a restriction upon their autonomy."

After reminding the Court that state power is no more to be used to handicap religion than to help it, he expressed another conviction not particularly present even in the dissenting opinions in the post-Everson series. "For there is involved in these cases a substantial free exercise claim on the part of those who affirmatively desire to have their children's school day open with the reading of passages from the Bible. It might also be argued that parents who want their children exposed to religious influences can adequately fulfill that wish off school property and outside school time. With all its surface persuasiveness, however, this argument seriously misconceives the basic constitutional justification for permitting the exercises at issue in these cases. For a compulsory state educational system so structures a child's life that if religious exercises are held to be an impermissible activity in schools, religion is placed at an artificial and state-created disadvantage. And a refusal to permit religious exercises thus is seen, not as the realization of state neutrality, but rather as the establishment of a religion of secularism or at the least, as government support of the beliefs of those who think that religious exercises should be conducted only in private. . . . What seems to me of paramount importance, then, is recognition of the fact that the claim advanced here in favor of Bible reading is sufficiently substantial to make simple reference to the constitutional phrase 'establishment of religion' as inadequate an analysis of the case before us as the ritualistic invocation of the non-constitutional phrase 'separation of church and state.'"

Justice Stewart then called for an analysis of the precise nature of that "neutrality" required by the interplay of the establishment and free-exercise clauses. He found in the present cases none of the danger to government or religion present in official support of instruction in the tenets of a particular sect. Since even teachers were not required to participate, he found not even an infinitesimal expenditure of public funds for the conducting of religious exercises. He found that in Abington Township no one translation of the Bible was required, and that in Baltimore another translation might be substituted for the King James version. He found no coercion upon those who did not choose to participate. "The governmental neutrality which the First and Fourteenth Amendments require in the cases before us, in other words, is the extension of even-handed treatment to all who believe, doubt, or disbelieve—a refusal on the part of the state to weight the scales of private choice. In these cases, therefore, what is involved is not state action based on impermissible categories, but rather an attempt by the state to accommodate those differences which the existence in our society of a variety of religious beliefs makes inevitable. The Constitution requires that such efforts be struck down only if they are proven to entail the use of the secular authority of government to coerce a preference among such beliefs. . . . What our Constitution indispensably protects is the freedom of each of us, be he Jew or agnostic, Christian or atheist, Buddhist or free-thinker, to believe or disbelieve, to worship or not worship, to pray or keep silent, according to his own conscience, uncoerced and unrestrained by the government. . . . I would remand both cases for further hearings."

It has been well said that one man in the right is a majority. It was true of Justice Stone in the Gobitis case, and ultimately the rights of a religious minority prevailed. It was true of Justice Reed in the McCollum case, and ultimately the compromise was effected which was a substantial vindication of his viewpoint. Let us at least not overlook the possibility that in 1963 it was Justice Stewart who spoke with the voice of the future.

The Court recognizes, as all thinking America recognized,

that with the Everson decision an entirely new day dawned in the American relationship of Church and State. It was no longer the *establishment* of religion that the First Amendment banned, but the establishment of *religion*. That was proclaimed alike in the majority and minority opinions; they differed only in the applicability of the principle to the specific problem presented by free bus rides for parochial school children. The Court, with Justice Stone dissenting, applied the principle in the McCollum case, banning released-time religious instruction in public school classrooms. It applied the principle again in the Engel case, banning the recitation of the Regents' prayer in the classrooms of New York. Once more the Court applied it, disappointing those who thought that a prayer attributed to Jesus might fare better than one sponsored by the New York Board of Regents, in the Schempp-Murray cases. It was a doctrine of absolute separation, of total barring of service by government to religion, that at least theoretically underlay all these decisions. Already the perils that always beset absolutism in any form are becoming apparent in this series of decisions.

SHALL THE MINORITY PREVAIL?

For one thing, the newly enunciated doctrine has had the practical result of bringing about minority rule where services to religion by public school systems are concerned. For some thirty years programs of released and dismissed time had been conducted in American schools without a challenge that reached the Supreme Court. Since the very birthday of American public education the recital of public prayers in classrooms had been a common practice, and time had long since hallowed the comparable practice of Bible reading. It is, to be sure, begging a question to refer to a long-established practice as a "right," but people tend to think of one as such. To most men in the street, "We always opened class with a prayer," implies as a self-evident corollary, "We have the right to do so now." In none of the cases in the McCollum to Schempp-Murray series was there evidence advanced of direct coercion upon the minority to participate in practices sanctioned by time and desired by the majority. At the most a sort of subtle, indirect coercion by example was charged, the sort of coercion that may be effective on some people but on others only gets their dander up. In no case was the minority right to abstain in question, but this did not satisfy the minority. The minority sued to make its will prevail, and it has substantially succeeded.

Ever since McCollum the preservation of minority rights has not been the issue; it has been the imposition upon the majority of minority rule. Justice Clark may say that the free-exercise clause "has never meant that a majority could use the machinery of the state to practice beliefs," but— assuming that the recitation of the Lord's Prayer or the reading aloud of the Bible is to practice a belief—the majority has done precisely that without challenge from the earliest days of public education. The assumption that a time-hallowed practice of dedicated and conscientious law-abiding Americans over many generations has been contrary to the fundamental law of their land without their ever suspecting it is not an assumption that commends itself to intellectual modesty. Those dissenting Justices who have repeatedly appealed to the traditions of the American people as themselves decisions by the supreme court of public opinion have a case. Ultimately the Constitution is not what the Supreme Court says it is. The Constitution is what the American people make it. Already voices are being heard calling for a constitutional amendment to make invalid the current Court's doctrine of "absolute separation," or "whole-some neutrality" in Justice Clark's mollifying phrase.

But more important are the implications of the doctrine of absolute separation in areas outside education. Justice Stewart pointed out the possible conflicts between the no-establishment clause and the free-exercise clause that can arise from the doctrinaire interpretation of the former. The Court has ruled out religious instruction and exercises in public school classrooms. Even in the latter Justice Stewart sees some conflict between the two clauses. It is a widely accepted custom to start the school day with the pledge of allegiance to the flag. Thereby the school day is conducted within a patriotic framework, and the Court once thought that framework so important that it took precedence over the religious scruples of the Jehovah's Witnesses. But if the simple repetition of the pledge of allegiance creates a patriotic framework of such importance, does not the simple repetition of the Lord's Prayer create a comparable religious framework? And is it not a limitation on the free exercise of religion to deny to religious-minded Americans—and they are the majority—the right to have their children educated within the framework?

But this is a point we do not wish to labor. The man in the street will hardly agree that the child is denied the free exercise of religion, as the phrase is ordinarily understood, by being denied the right to start the school day with the Lord's Prayer. But let us follow the logic of the situation into other areas, as Justice Stewart did.

A child is partially removed from his free milieu by re-quired attendance at school. A person in the armed services is much more removed, and a person in a public hospital or penal institution is totally removed. Custom has sancti-fied the conducting of religious services for such people on the sensible grounds that government should make available to them the "pastoral guidance," in Justice Stewart's phrase, which they could freely seek in a free milieu. Specifically, there are chapels in military installations and hospitals; chaplains hold commissions in the armed services and are on the public payroll. Denominational services are held at army posts, public hospitals, and penal institutions; and the taxpayer pays the bill.

If a religious class in a public school classroom is an establishment of religion, then surely a denominational service on an army post is an establishment of religion. If the recitation of the Lord's Prayer in a classroom is an establishment of religion, then surely a denominational service in a public hospital or jail is an establishment of religion. If the former are unconstitutional, and the Supreme Court under its doctrine of absolute separation has said that they are, then how could the latter stand up under Court scrutiny? Logically the chaplains should be dismissed from the armed services and clergymen denied entrance to public hospitals and jails to render the consolations of religion to those behind their walls. Americans should die on the field of battle or in hospital rooms, and the word of God be barred from the battlefield and the hospital room because the utterance of it under public sponsorship violates the no-establishment clause of the First Amendment.

If one wishes to follow logic any further, and fortunately for the success of society few people do, then the doctrinaire interpretation of the no-establishment clause comes into direct conflict with even a latitudinarian interpretation of the free-exercise clause. Certainly there would be a positive violation by the state of the right to the free exercise of religion if a man dying in a public hospital were denied the final consolations of his faith because to receive them would violate the constitutional prohibition on the establishment of religion.

The conclusion is inescapable. A doctrinaire interpretation of either clause would render inoperative the other clause. If a total separation of Church and State could be effected, it would deny to the no small number of Americans who are withdrawn from their ordinary free milieus the free exercise of their religions. If the free exercise of religion were made paramount beyond challenge, all sorts of situations might result which would make meaningless the prohibition against the establishment of religion. The truth is that the one clause must be accommodated to the other, by the rule of reason and justice. But that is really all that the dissenting Justices have been saying ever since Justice Reed dissented in the McCollum case.

Bibliographical Note

The obvious work with which to open a bibliographical note on the American relations of Church and State is Canon Anson Phelps Stokes's three-volume study, *Church and State in the United States* (New York, 1950), to which this and every contemporary treatment of the subject must be indebted at all points within the area stated in its title. Comparably invaluable for the European backgrounds of the American relationship is the series edited by F. J. C. Hearnshaw, *The Social and Political Ideas of Some Great Mediaeval Thinkers* (New York, 1950), *The Social and Political Ideas of Some Great Thinkers of the Renaissance and the Reformation* (New York, n.d.), and *The Social and Political Ideas of Some Great Thinkers of the Sixteenth and Seventeenth Centuries* (New York, 1939).

For the medieval theory of Church and State (Ch. 1) William Archibald Dunning, *A History of Political Theories Ancient and Medieval* (New York, 1923) is valuable, as is J. W. Allen, *A History of Political Thought in the Sixteenth Century* (London, 1928) for the general Renaissance and Reformation background (Ch. 2). Other general treatments of the political and social thought of the period of Reformation are Sylvia Benians, *From Renaissance to*

Reformation (New York, 1923) and Henry Osborn Taylor, *Thought and Expression in the Sixteenth Century* (2d ed., rev., New York, 1930).

For Luther's influence (Ch. 2), L. H. Waring, *The Political Theories of Martin Luther* (New York, 1910), is directly on our theme. H. E. Jacobs, *Martin Luther* (New York, 1898), T. M. Lindsay, *Luther and the German Reformation* (Edinburgh, 1900), and R. H. Murray, *Erasmus and Luther* (London, 1920) also are useful. See Allen's sixteenth-century volume for Melanchthon and Calvin; Taylor is especially useful on Calvin. For the influence of Calvin on democracy the lecture by Rev. W. R. Matthews, Dean of King's College, in Hearnshaw's Renaissance and Reformation volume is particularly informing. Also on Calvin, A. Mitchell Hunter, *The Teaching of Calvin* (Glasgow, 1920), Alan Menzies, *A Study of Calvin* (London, 1918), and Hugh Y. Reyburn, *John Calvin* (London, 1904). For Knox, see Allen; also Edwin Muir, *John Knox, Portrait of a Calvinist* (New York, 1929). References to Knox's *Appellation* are to his *The Appellation of John Knox from the Cruel and Most Unjust Sentence Pronounced Against Him by the Bishoppes and Clergie of Scotland, with His Supplication and Exhortation to the Nobilitie, Estates and Communaltie of the Same Realm* (1558) in *The Works of John Knox*, ed. David Laing (8 vols., Edinburgh, 1846–64), Vol. IV.

For the position of Henry VIII on the issue (Ch. 3), see Allen, especially Ch. IV of Part II. The best contemporary expression of Henry's final position is to be found in the work of Christopher St. German, *An Answere to a Letter* and *Treatise Concerning the Division Between the Spiritualitie and the Temporalities* (c. 1532). For Elizabeth, see Allen, Ch. V of Part II, and Hearnshaw, *The Social and Political Ideas of Some Great Thinkers of the Sixteenth and Seventeenth Centuries*, Ch. I, "Introductory: the Social and Political Problems of the Sixteenth and Seventeenth Centuries," by the editor. For the Puritans in England, see Allen, Hearnshaw, and George Peabody Gooch, *English Democratic Ideas in the Seventeenth Century* (Cambridge, 1927), especially Chs. II and III.

Scholarly writing on the Massachusetts colonies and their philosophy (Ch. 4) is enormous in scope. Roland G. Usher, *The Pilgrims and Their History* (New York, 1918), and Perry Miller and Thomas H. Johnson, *The Puritans* (New York, 1938) may be mentioned. For the Church of England in America (Ch. 5), Arthur Lyon Cross, *The Anglican Episcopate and the American Colonies* (New York,

1902) is especially useful for the light shed on religious conditions and relations in the South. For the middle colonies (Ch. 6), William Warren Sweet, *Religion in Colonial America* (New York, 1942), Frederick J. Zwierlein, *Religion in New Netherland* (Rochester, N.Y., 1910), James Bowden, *The History of the Society of Friends in America* (2 vols., London, 1850), and Sydney G. Fisher, *The Quaker Colonies* (Yale University Press, 1921).

For The Battle of the Bishops (Ch. 7) see Cross; Sweet, Ch. II; and Sanford H. Cobb, *The Rise of Religious Liberty in America* (New York, 1902), Ch. VIII. For the Great Awakening in the South (Ch. 8), W. M. Gewehr, *The Great Awakening in Virginia, 1740–90* (Durham, N.C., 1930). For the specific contributions of Jonathan Edwards, H. B. Parkes, *Jonathan Edwards, The Fiery Puritan* (New York, 1930) and A. C. McGiffert, *Jonathan Edwards* (New York, 1932); for Whitefield, Edward S. Ninde, *George Whitefield, Prophet-Preacher* (New York, c. 1924).

The pertinent state constitution texts (Ch. 9) may be found in B. P. Poore, *The Federal and State Constitutions, Colonial Charters, and Other Organic Laws of the United States* (2 vols., Washington, 1877) and in Francis Newton Thorpe, *The Federal and State Constitutions, Colonial Charters, and Organic Laws of the States, Territories, and Colonies Now or Heretofore Forming the United States of America* (7 vols., Washington, 1909).

A good general treament of the disestablishment process is Rev. Joseph F. Thorning, S.J., *Religious Liberty in Transition* (New York, 1931). The New England record (Ch. 10) is discussed in Chs. II (Massachusetts), III (Connecticut), and V (New Hampshire). Also of interest are Anson Eli Morse, *The Federalist Party in Massachusetts to the Year 1800* (Princeton University Press, 1909), and M. Louise Greene, *The Development of Religious Liberty in Connecticut* (New York, 1905).

No single study is devoted to the process of disestablishment outside New England (Ch. 11). The pertinent constitutional documents of New Jersey and Pennsylvania may be found in Thorpe, Vol. V, and of Maryland in Vol. III. On the Maryland struggle for the civil rights of Jews, see E. Milton Altfeld, *The Jew's Struggle for Religious and Civil Liberty in Maryland* (Baltimore, 1924). For South Carolina see Ch. X of Allan Nevins, *The American States During and After the Revolution* (New York, 1927).

Charles Warren, *The Supreme Court in United States History* (Boston, 1923) is fundamental for the earlier interpretation of the

Fourteenth Amendment (Ch. 12). Charles W. Collins, *The Fourteenth Amendment and the States* (New York, 1912) is also valuable for the earlier period. Contrasting appraisals of the contributions of Justice Stephen J. Field to the process may be found in a contemporary, conservative interpretation by Chauncy F. Black and Samuel B. Smith, *Some Account of the Work of Stephen J. Field as a Legislator, State Judge, and Judge of the Supreme Court of the United States* (New York, 1881) and a modern, liberal interpretation by Robert Green McCloskey, *American Conservatism in the Age of Enterprise* (Harvard University Press, 1951).

In the citation of Supreme Court decisions (Chs. 13 and 14), the name of the case comes first, then the volume number of *United States Reports*, followed by the first page of the report (e.g., *Munn v. Illinois,* 94 U.S. 113). The same system of citation is used in state court reports. The common abbreviations are U.S. (*United States Reports*); et al. (*et alii;* "and others"); ex rel. (*ex relatione;* "at the information of"); and v. (*versus;* "against").

Among the better general studies of the Church and State relationship as defined by the Supreme Court in twentieth-century cases are Loren P. Beth, *American Theory of Church and State* (University of Florida Press, 1958); Evarts B. Greene, *Religion and the State: the Making and Testing of an American Tradition* (New York University Press, 1941); Mark de Wolfe Howe, *Cases on Church and State in the United States* (Harvard University Press, 1952); Alvin W. Johnson and Frank H. Yost, *Separation of Church and State in the United States* (University of Minnesota Press, 1948); Leo Pfeffer, *Church, State and Freedom* (Boston, 1953); William G. Torpey, *Judicial Doctrines of Religious Rights in America* (University of North Carolina Press, 1948); Joseph Tussman, *The Supreme Court on Church and State* (Oxford University Press, 1962); and Virginia Wood, "Separation of Church and State," in *Due Process of Law: 1932–1949; The Supreme Court's Use of a Constitutional Tool* (Louisiana State University Press, 1951). The legal aspects are best studied through Carl F. G. Zollman, *American Church Law* (St. Paul, Minn., 1933) and Wilber G. Katz, "Religion and Law in America," in James W. Smith and A. Leland Jamison, eds., *Religious Perspectives in American Culture* (Religion in American Life, vol. 2; Princeton University Press, 1961).

The Supreme Court opinions are readily available, in adequate excerpt, in the following cases: Oregon parochial school, Louisiana textbook, New Jersey bus, Barnette flag salute, McCollum released

time, and Zorach dismissed time in David Fellman, ed., *The Supreme
Court and Education* (Teachers College, Columbia University, 1960).

The full record of *Meyer* v. *State of Nebraska* is to be found in
Arthur F. Mullen, *Western Democrat* (New York, 1940; pp. 206–26)
and Orville H. Zabel, *God and Caesar in Nebraska* (University of
Nebraska Press, 1955; pp. 130–59). For *Pierce* v. *Society of Sisters*
(the Oregon parochial school case), see Richard L. Neuberger, *Our
Promised Land* (New York, 1938; Ch. VI, "Government by the
People"). The entire record has been published as *Oregon School
Cases* (Baltimore, 1925). The Gobitis and Barnette decisions (Jeho-
vah's Witnesses flag-salute cases) are treated in Jerre S. Williams,
The Supreme Court Speaks (University of Texas Press, 1956; Part 6),
as are the Everson and Zorach decisions (New Jersey bus and dismissed-time cases). A comprehensive study of Bible reading in public
schools is available in Donald E. Boles, *The Bible, Religion, and the
Public Schools* (Iowa State University Press, 1963).

For the very extensive literature on the Everson, McCollum, and
Zorach cases, reference may be made to Brother Edmond G. Drouin,
*The School Question: a Bibliography on Church-State of Relation-
ships in American Education, 1940–60* (Catholic University of America Press, 1963), which is comprehensive for the period indicated in
the subtitle and valuable for the earlier period.

Notes

CHAPTER I

1. Mansi, *Sacrorum conciliorum collectio,* VIII, 31.

2. Lorenz Jaeger, Archbishop of Paderborn, *The Ecumenical Council, The Church and Christendom,* tr. by A. V. Littledale, New York, Kenedy, 1962, p. 23.

3. Quoted in William A. Dunning, *A History of Political Theories Ancient and Medieval,* New York, Macmillan, 1923, pp. 22, 224–25.

4. *Defensor,* I, 12, tr. by Dunning, *op. cit.,* p. 239.

CHAPTER II

1. Ed. by Abel Lanfranc, Paris, H. Champion, 1911, p. 755.

2. *Institutes,* 1559 ed., lib. IV, p. 374.

3. *Ibid.,* II, iii, Ch. 19.

4. *Ibid.,* II, iv, p. 528.

5. *Appellation,* in *Works,* ed. by David Laing, 8 vols., Edinburgh, 1846–64; IV, p. 416.

6. *Ibid.,* IV, pp. 495–96.

7. *Ibid.,* IV, p. 501.

8. *History of the Reformation in Scotland,* Laing, ed., Edinburgh, 2 vols., The Woodrow Society, II, p. 442.

CHAPTER III

1. 1557 ed., pp. 185–86.

2. In *Chronicles,* Hall, 1548, pp. 261–62.

3. *Complaynt of Roderyck Mors,* Geneva, 1542, Ch. 14.

4. *An Admonition to England and Scotland to call them to repentance* (published with Knox's *Appellation*).

5. *Life and Manners of all true Christians,* Middleburgh, 1582, p. 2.

6. *Ibid.,* Definition 25.

CHAPTER IV

1. *Ne Sutor ultra Crepidam,* Boston, 1681, p. 4.

2. For Winthrop's speech, see Miller and Johnson, *The Puritans,* New York, American Book Company, 1938, pp. 206–7.

CHAPTER V

1. Hening, *Statutes,* I, pp. 122–24.

2. Bishop Sherlock, "Report on the State of the Church of England in the Colonies," *New York Documents,* VII, p. 361.

3. *State Papers, Domestic Series,* Charles I, No. 247, October 1–15, 1633.

CHAPTER VI

1. *Ecclesiastical Records of the State of New York,* 7 vols., Albany, 1901–1916, I, p. 152.

2. Rochester, New York, 1910.

3. *Ecclesiastical Records of the State of New York,* II, pp. 864–65.

4. Cf. William Warren Sweet, *Religion in Colonial America,* New York, Scribner's, 1942, p. 209.

5. Quoted in James Bowden, *The History of the Society of Friends in America,* 2 vols., London, 1850, I, p. 320.

CHAPTER VII

1. *Letters of Robert Carter,* ed. by Louis B. Wright, Huntington Library, San Marino, California, 1940. Quoted in Sweet, *Religion in Colonial America,* p. 71.

2. Letter to H. Niles, Feb. 13, 1818, *Works,* X, p. 288.

CHAPTER VIII

1. *Jonathan Edwards*, 1703–1758, New York, Macmillan, 1940, p. 181.

CHAPTER IX

1. Hening, *Statutes*, XI, iii. Quoted in Sanford H. Cobb, *The Rise of Religious Liberty in America*, New York, Macmillan, 1902, pp. 491–92.

2. Quoted in Cobb, *ibid.*, p. 498.

CHAPTER X

1. *Writings of Thomas Jefferson*, Monticello ed., XVI, pp. 281–82.

2. *Journal of the Convention, Sept. 1, 1779 to June 16, 1780*, Boston, 1832, pp. 263–64.

3. B. P. Poore, *Federal and State Constitutions*, Washington, D.C., 2 vols., 1877; Government Printing Office, I, pp. 957–58.

4. Poore, *loc. cit.*

5. *Journal of the Convention*, pp. 218, 220.

6. Edward Buck, *Massachusetts Ecclesiastical Law*, Boston, 1866, p. 40.

7. Anson Eli Morse, *The Federalist Party in Massachusetts to the Year 1800*, Princeton, The University Library, 1909, pp. 147–48.

8. *Autobiography and Correspondence*, ed. by Charles Beecher, New York, 1864, I, pp. 517–18.

9. Poore, *op. cit.*, I, p. 975.

10. *The Rights of Conscience therefore Religious Opinions not cognizable by Law; or, The High-flying Church-man*. Quoted in M. Louise Greene, *The Development of Religious Liberty in Connecticut*, Boston and New York, Houghton Mifflin, 1905, pp. 374–76.

11. *Collections of the New Hampshire Historical Society*, Concord, New Hampshire, VIII, p. 5.

12. *Journal of the New Hampshire House*, November 1804, p. 63.

13. John N. McClintock, *History of New Hampshire*, Boston, B. B. Russell, p. 52.

CHAPTER XI

1. Francis Newton Thorpe, *The Federal and State Constitutions*, 7 vols., Washington, Government Printing Office, 1909, V, pp. 2597–98.

2. *Ibid.*, V, p. 2599, Art. I, 4.

3. *Ibid.*, V, p. 3085.

4. *Ibid.*, V, p. 3100.

5. *Ibid.*, III, p. 1690.

6. E. Milton Altfeld, *The Jew's Struggle for Religious and Civil Liberty in Maryland*, Baltimore, M. Curlander, 1924, p. 10.

7. *Ibid.*, pp. 52–53.

CHAPTER XII

1. Congressional Globe, 39th Congress, 1st session, May 10, 1866, pp. 2542–43.

CHAPTER XIII

1. Quoted in Anson Phelps Stokes, *Church and State in the United States*, 3 vols., New York, Harper, 1950, II, p. 741.

2. *Our Promised Land*, New York, Macmillan, 1938, Ch. 6.

3. Charles Warren, *The Supreme Court in United States History*, Boston, Little Brown, 3 vols., 1923, p. 458.

CHAPTER XIV

1. Alvin W. Johnson, *Legal Status of Church-State Relationships in the United States*, Minneapolis, University of Minnesota Press, 1934, pp. 143, 145.

Index